Losing Cissie, Saving Myself

*The Perils of Caring for My Wife
Through Her Memory Loss*

Peter Barnet

Library of Congress Cataloging-in-Publication Data

Peter Barnet, Losing Cissie, Saving Myself: The Perils of Caring for My
Wife Through Her Memory Loss, dementia, Alzheimer disease, aging,
caregiving.

Summary: A husband's loving memoir of his marriage and struggles with
the challenges of caring for his wife as she struggles with dementia.

ISBN: 978-1-939282-47-7

Published by Miniver Press, LLC, McLean Virginia
Copyright 2020 Peter Barnet

First edition November 2020

Table of Contents

Introduction

The American Hospital of Paris

March 17, 2017, 7:00 pm

"How much time do we have?" I asked.

"Three–four years, maybe more, maybe less," the neurologist replied.

"How will it evolve?"

"It is difficult to say because everyone is different. In time she will likely lose all her languages except Swedish."

"Then I won't be able to talk with her."

"You will have to learn Swedish."

"But how can she lose English? She has been speaking it every day for over fifty years. We are an Anglophone home. Her English is almost as good as mine."

"Your wife will lose her English and her French and her German. It does not matter how long or how well she speaks them today. They are not stored in the same place in her brain as her native language...and she might even lose it, but that is rare."

"Should I take her to Stockholm? Should we move there?"

"It would be better for her, certainly more comfortable to be in her own language and culture. Yes, it's a good idea."

"And you are certain she has Alzheimer's?"

"After the PET Scan last week, I am ninety-five percent sure. The only way to be one hundred percent sure is an autopsy after death."

"Will you tell my wife?"

"Only if she asks me directly. If she doesn't, I simply describe Alzheimer's as a memory disease. The word is terrifying so why put her through that? And she will forget it in one or two days anyway."

The doctor wasn't finished. He paused, and then leaned forward in his chair to continue. "Monsieur Barnet, I am so sorry, but you must prepare yourself for an even more difficult time ahead. You are most of all going to have to take care of yourself. Alzheimer's is actually more dangerous for you than it is for your wife. Almost two-thirds of primary care giving spouses die before the afflicted one. Stress is a killer in old people. And you are going to be facing an incredible amount of it over the coming months and years. You're going to have to find ways to deal with it—or you may very well die before your wife."

His remark struck me hard. It sums up the terrible quandary for growing millions of elder people like myself—loving caregivers to spouses who are victims of dementia and Alzheimer's.

In a way we need more aid than our afflicted spouses. At this point, medicine can do very little but delay their fate...and even that is uncertain. We, on the other hand, must care for our spouses, while at the same time avert the fate that could be in store for us if we do nothing to deal with our own situation.

It is for that reason that I chose to write this book—as a tale of my wonderful life with a marvelous woman—but at the same time a primer on what a caring spouse can do to aid their better half, and at the same time to prolong their own life.

Chapter 1

Early Signs

Paris, July 2014

Scientists often treat patients as objects when describing diseases. But Alzheimer's is an emotional drama for caregivers and best understood when told with the patient and spouse as subjects, as individuals.

Almost three years before that fateful diagnosis described above, I began to wonder if something was going on with Cissie. There was nothing specific and indeed we were getting older but she just seemed less sharp and even a bit fragile at times. I convinced myself it was just my imagination. However, I couldn't shake this thought.

Her Pan Am alumni group arranged a Bastille Day, 14th of July party at a member's apartment to watch the fireworks. Cissie had written down the door code to enter the building and the time. Most residential buildings in Paris have security code entrances. It was common for guests to get them wrong. And this had already happened several times in recent months. In fact, it was happening regularly.

We arrived at the address. Cissie gave me the code to open the door. It did not work. So, we decided to wait for the next person to arrive for the party but no one came. Cissie telephoned another member to ask for the code and double check the start time of the party. She passed the phone to me. We were an hour early and Cissie had transposed two of the four numbers of the door code.

Later at the party a woman assured me she had given the right code to Cissie on the phone but had to repeat herself several times before Cissie got it right and wrote it down correctly. She was a bit irritated. Cissie had not written it down correctly.

We went on summer holiday and had a nice time but Cissie did not feel well a lot. She had begun to suffer from acid reflux which sometimes laid her up for one or two days. We bought the usual antacids including maximum strength varieties and then tried prescription ones. None really relieved her discomfort. But again, this is very common. Nevertheless, my worries were growing.

As the summer and fall progressed it seemed that Cissie had less energy. I chalked this up to aging; we were now 71 and afternoon naps and early nights were part of life for us. Yet she was spending more and more time in bed.

One day Cissie asked me for help. She was working on her investments. The stock market had become an interest to her. She asked me the following question: "I bought this stock at $85 and today it is at $112. How do I figure out what percent gain that is?"

So, I showed her.

She said thanks and went back to her desk.

I didn't like that. We learn to calculate percentages at an early age. This is basic arithmetic.

Cissie was a math whiz at school but she had forgotten how to do this. My worries increased further. But again, I thought that perhaps this was just age.

I also began to hear rumblings from her girlfriends in her ladies' conversation group that Cissie seemed less interested at their weekly meetings and often interrupted others with out-of-the-blue comments unrelated to the conversation in progress. They thought something was wrong. Cissie was usually outspoken but not so much anymore.

She told me that she was tired of the group. The conversations had become boring. I heard by the grapevine that her new friend from our temporary apartment wondered whether Cissie was hard of hearing. She seemed to repeat herself and asked the same questions time and again. Now I was really worried but not yet truly alarmed.

The jangling wakeup call came in March 2015. I had retired from The American University of Paris the previous semester and contracted to teach two courses at the American Business School in the fall. I was now at home a lot. There is an old joke about marriage and retirement. The wife says to her husband: "I married you for better or worse but not for lunch." Cissie did not like having me at home during the day and frankly, I didn't like being home either. This was an adjustment for both of us.

One morning Cissie asked me when I was going to teach again. I answered, "In the fall."

She reacted with enthusiasm: "Oh great, that's only a couple of weeks from now."

I repeated, "I said in the fall."

She returned, "Well it's August, isn't it. So that's a couple of weeks from now."

I froze and then replied, "Sweetie, it's March."

She said, a little nonplussed, "Oh," and left the room.

Now I was alarmed.

In May, we invited our new American friends from the temporary apartment to the Swedish Club for a jazz evening and a light supper. We reserved a good table for four, ordered some wine, and chatted together. Cissie excused herself to go to the powder room, and when she was gone, our lady friend said to me, "Peter, I love Cissie. I only wish I had met her twenty years ago so I could have enjoyed our friendship longer. We have decided to get a place in Washington D.C. and want you to move there, too. I want Cissie near me because I want to take care of her as she gets older."

I looked at her and all I could say was, "I love you."

The next morning, I called our friend and asked her why she had said what she said the evening before. Of course, I knew the answer but wanted to hear it in case I misunderstood.

She replied, "Cissie brought me lunch last week when I was down with the flu. She was unusually scattered. She asked me the same question three times in twenty minutes and told me again about the book she is reading. She tells me that every time we see each other as if it were the first time. We've seen this before in another friend and fear where this is going. I want to be there for Cissie."

I hung up and called my doctor for a recommendation to a neurologist. I had put this off long enough. It was time.

I took Cissie to our first appointment with a neurologist at The American Hospital of Paris in September 2015. She came without fuss. I think she knew something was wrong. He asked her opening questions as to the day, week, month, and season. She got about half of the answers right. When we had finished, he said Cissie was suffering from a "mild cognitive impairment." It was not serious and could just be age but he ordered a MRI of her hippocampus. That's the memory zone of the brain.

He further prescribed a cognition test with an "autophonist," a language professional who gives these verbal and drawing tests for neurologists. Again, Cissie took the cognition test (about ninety minutes long) without complaint. She always liked and excelled at tests. She did not excel at this one.

The MRI showed mild atrophy of her hippocampus. This can be normal in a 72-year-old. All older people develop memory problems. The cognition test confirmed mild impairment. The doctor wanted to see Cissie in one year.

I asked him privately how long she would have if this were indeed Alzheimer's disease. He told me the malady progresses very slowly. She had at least another four years before she would become incompetent and the average life expectancy for Alzheimer's victims was seven years after diagnosis. He cautioned that there was no way of knowing what her trouble was at this early stage. Alzheimer's, he said is very difficult to diagnose and all cases are individual.

We went home and returned to normal life. Cissie asked me few questions about my private meeting with the doctor, which I thought was unlike her at the time.

It was early days for me, too.

Chapter 2

Summa Cum Laude (Cissie's Story)

On February 24, 1943, Cissie was born Maj Sigrid Ekvall in Gothenburg, Sweden...and the gods must have smiled. Cissie did not look like Winston Churchill. He was British Prime Minister at the time and claimed with some accuracy that all babies looked like him, little cherubs and not so easy to distinguish.

And the gods further smiled because they could see ahead to an exceptionally beautiful and very bright girl. Her maternal grandfather who had migrated to Sweden from the then Austro-Hungarian Empire nicknamed her Cissie after Sissi, the young 19th century empress but had the good taste to change the "S" to a "C" to avoid it being too kitsch. The nickname stuck and Cissie was launched.

When I met her thirty-two years later I would describe her looks to buddies as Grace Kelly–like or Ingrid Thulin one of Ingmar Bergman's ingénues. When they would meet her they always reacted with wonder and awe:

"How did you catch that?"

And after we married: "That's your wife?"

The gods smiled on me, too for different reasons...but I get ahead of myself.

Cissie started life with her parents in a suburban house that her father had literally built with another guy in 1935. He bought the whole thing as a kit for $5000 and the two of them put it together. Sound familiar? Another Swedish fellow would start IKEA some years later.

Cissie was a happy child doing what happy suburban children do: riding her bike, playing with her dolls, hugging her cat named

Pele, and playing with her friends at school and in the neighborhood. Her mother was a talented seamstress who made a lot of her clothes. When they went into the city, Cissie would sing to the passengers on the trolley and sometimes they clapped. Her dad was an executive at Volvo and therefore drove a car at a time when few Swedes had one. Cissie was very proud of her dad and his car. He would take the family on outings and vacations in it.

Cissie excelled at school. She earned straight As, and as she grew, demonstrated an independent and willful spirit. If she set her mind on doing something, she would do it. If she did not want to do something she wouldn't. If she liked another student she would show it; if she didn't like someone she would show that, too. She was never shy about voicing opinions and engaging others in disagreements. She was blossoming into a beauty with brains who stood her ground but loved her friends and loved to have fun. She was popular and her girlfriends were very important to her. She was growing into both an intellectual and social animal. The gods smiled.

And then, they didn't.

When Cissie was 12, her father lost his job and the harmony in her family collapsed. The stresses and recriminations were such that her parents soon divorced, unpleasantly. Her mother was forced to sell their suburban house and take a modest apartment in Gothenburg. Cissie had to change schools and most of her friends. Her mother went back to work. Her father pretty much disappeared into exile.

Divorce does not exactly have a reputation of being good for children and many say it is particularly tough on young teenage girls. It was very tough on Cissie but it also made her tough, strong, independent, critical, and determined to excel. Her mother recognized her strengths and drove her to keep up the straight As, be careful about "the boys," and set ambitious life goals.

At 16 she met prince charming at a school dance. She danced divinely and this caught his eye. He was 24 and the scion of one of Gothenburg's leading families. He was also a gentleman.

At the end of the evening, he gave Cissie his card somewhat formally and asked: "When is your birthday?" She told him and he then went on: "When you turn eighteen on February 24 two years from now, I will call and ask you out. Until then, grow up well."

Cissie was impressed but wondered if this good-looking prince was just toying wth her. He wasn't. She did not hear from him until the promised day. On her 18th birthday, Sven called, congratulated her and asked her to have dinner with him. She accepted and her mother almost had a stroke. Sven's mother was a German countess and his father was the owner of a major business.

They dated for three years during Cissie's university studies. She graduated second in her class from Gothenburg Handelshule (business school). But now she faced a decision. She could get a job locally and probably marry Sven who by then had inherited his family business and considerable wealth. That might be wonderful but it came with a price: a life in Gothenburg. She wanted to see the world, broaden her horizons, and had little interest in marrying so young.

So she decided to join SAS Airlines as a stewardess. This was very prestigious in those days. SAS based her in Copenhagen and she began to see the world. Two years later she joined Pan American in New York. Pan Am was in its heyday. It paid very well, literally flew worldwide, and Pan Am stewardesses were like rock stars.

And so, in February 1967 it was goodbye to Scandinavia, Gothenburg, and Sven, who by then had met someone else. They would remain friends and he would come back into our lives. But for Cissie, now 24, it was the Big Apple, USA, and pretty much all of planet earth. Maj Sigrid Ekvall had spread her wings, literally. The gods were smiling.

Trying out the new Jumbo 747 engine

...

Paris, Charles de Gaulle Airport, January 2018

Cissie and I settled into our seats and I asked the attendant for a double bourbon.

Cissie looked at me. "Isn't that a bit heavy for a morning flight?"

"Not today, dear," I replied.

She was oblivious to what she had put me through. But then again, why wouldn't she be. By 2018, she was in the grip of Alzheimer's.

Air France had upgraded us to business class on the Paris–Miami flight. We were delighted, even excited. But then Cissie remembered miraculously that she had hated our business class return flight from Florida the previous year. I had upgraded our seats to make her comfortable on the night flight. That had not worked out well because she had found their new mini cabin configuration isolating and her full reclining seat uncomfortable.

As we approached security, Cissie asked me if the seats would be the same as last year. I had no idea and told her so. This flight was on the double-decker Airbus 380. We got up to the scanner with hand luggage already on its way through, when she announced, "I am not going. You can go by yourself. I'm going home."

She refused to move forward. Others in the cue became annoyed. I begged and cajoled her to no effect. She had dug in her heels. Appeals to logic and social embarrassment did not work. Our bags were checked; we had gone through border control, our hand luggage was on the other side of the scanner, and we were holding up the line.

"I am not going," she repeated, "you can go alone."

I thought I was going to have a stroke. Finally, I said, "We'll change our seats back to premium economy at the Air France Lounge"

"Do you promise?"

"Yes, I promise. I swear to you we will get our old seats back."

"All right, but if we don't get them back, I am not going."

We went through the scanner and proceeded to the lounge. I was totally stressed as we walked there through the departures area. I thought I was going to come apart. This was way beyond frustration and there was no time for depression during this drama. I was genuinely frantic. I felt as if my heart was in my mouth and that my whole body was on fire. This could not go on. I thought I was on the verge of hysteria.

The Air France man at the reception desk looked at me with incredulity. "I've never heard of anyone wanting to downgrade. You were upgraded because you are a Flying Blue Platinum for Life card member. This is our way of rewarding our most loyal customers. Business class is wonderful on our Airbus 380. It would be a shame for Madame and you to miss it. And I see your old seats have been reassigned. There are no places left in premium economy. I could give you economy seats in the very back of the plane."

I asked the man to show us the 380 business class configurations. It had the traditional side-by-side seats. Our two were in the center between aisles.

We showed them to Cissie and she felt better. She agreed to go. The Air France man looked relieved. I'm certain he could not begin to imagine how I felt, frantic and embarrassed at the same time...I was exhausted.

I went back to thank him for his professionalism and patience before we boarded the flight. He thanked me and suggested in a most polite, even gracious manner that I had an "interesting" wife.

Cissie in her Pan Am uniform

New York, February 1967

During her Pan Am years (1967–1977), Cissie saw the world's museums and churches, and the great cultural sites across five continents. She shopped at fashion boutiques by day and danced at the most famous discotheques at night. She particularly loved New Jimmy's in Paris and famous ones in Teheran and Beirut before their revolution and civil war.

She stayed at Intercontinental Hotels (owned by Pan Am) and other fine ones around the world. She often had two-three day or longer layovers in marvelous tourist destinations and she flew into Cambodia and Vietnam during the war. She had a Swiss boyfriend in Bangkok and he helped her select and ship some spectacular Thai chairs to New York. We still have one. With her air passes on the airline she showed her mother the world.

Cissie loved to travel. She had become a globetrotter.

She preferred working in first class rather than economy. There were fewer passengers; they were more elegant and better dressed and the food service was sensational. "Much more interesting," she would say than "the cattle car service" in the back. Her favorite plane was the new Boeing 747.

Cissie had many stories to tell over the years and she adored swapping them with other stewardess alumni years later in Paris. One of her favorites was about a night flight from New York to Rome with a stop over in Paris. An impossibly obnoxious and rude travel agent who was flying first class for free so irritated another passenger that he got up when Cissie was serving a cherries jubilee desert, took the cherry sauce bowl from her, and poured the whole thing over the guy's head. That doesn't happen every day!

Cissie had many adventures and she had many beaus who pursued her but she was very choosey. Her beauty kept growing and growing, her wardrobe was spectacular, not because she was rich but because she saved her money. Her fashion philosophy was: "better to have a few high quality items than a lot of so-so stuff." She lived by that. She did not like men because they had wealth; she liked them because they were interesting and fun and genuinely nice. She had a ball.

After several years, the glamour was wearing off a bit and she wanted new experiences. She applied for business jobs in Manhattan, primarily at banks. She was shocked to discover that

American companies did not recognize her university degree, as her Swedish one was based on three rather than four years of study. No one bothered to ask about her baccalaureate from high school, which is equivalent to one more year than American secondary education. They do today.

So Cissie went back to college to complete the last year for a US bachelor degree. She went to Fordham University in New York whilst still flying full time. She was senior enough by then to pick her preferred routes. She virtually commuted between New York and Buenos Aires because she could schedule these flights for the nights she did not have class—they were twelve hours in length and she could study for hours after the passengers had gone to sleep.

Cissie took sixteen business courses and scored a perfect 4.0 in each. She graduated one week before our wedding with the highest academic honor for an American Degree: Summa Cum Laude.

...

Paris, January 2019

Three nights before Cissie went into the hospital, I attended a board meeting to get away. Cissie's Swedish companion came over and cooked dinner for them both. They had a nice time and watched television together. When I got home, Cissie was calm and smiling.

She said to her friend, "Peter is the new man in my life. I am so incredibly fortunate to meet such a wonderful man at my age. I'm so glad we met." Then she added, "He's not at all like that jerk I was married to in New York."

Peter Barnet

Chapter 3

Mad Man (Peter's Story)

I was born May 9, 1943 in Washington D.C. It was wartime; my father was a junior naval officer who shipped out to the Pacific ten days later. He was Yale educated and a son of privilege. He ended the war on the staff of the chief of naval operations and was offered a transfer to the regular Navy and a jump of two clicks to full commander if he would make the service his career. He was only twenty-six and loved the Navy.

My mother did not and "lowered the boom." It would be the Navy or her but not both. He chose her. So we moved to New York City and a career in publishing for him, a private boys school for my younger brother and me. Our mom was a modern postwar American housewife in her habits, including ordering groceries by phone for home delivery. (That convenience did not prevail but is now back in our digital age.)

Somehow, given apartment living and the temple of convenience to which my mother was devout, I arrived at age 10 believing that vegetables were grown frozen by Birds Eye. I was very skinny and only liked fried chicken and chocolate ice cream.

And then life changed. My father got a job as publisher of the Paris Edition of The New York Herald Tribune (as it was named in the 1950s). We moved to Paris and into a rented house in the suburb of Garches. On our first day my mother took us to a café in the town for lunch. As a family we probably knew only three French words between us: bonjour, si vous plait, and merci. So what transpired was the result of sign language.

The café was small, modest looking, and crowded with men covered in dust from their construction jobs next door. The one waitress made it clear after many hand signals that there was no menu and we had two choices: we could have lunch or we could not have lunch. We took the first choice and after some time she served us a veal chop in a cream sauce, with string beans and sautéed potatoes. Both my brother and I took one bite and in excited unison said: "Mommy, this is gooood." In my memory, that was the day I discovered food and I have been devoted to it ever since.

We stayed two years in France and the experience was profound for a now-budding adolescent. I loved Paris, its architecture, its charm, and its rhythm. I loved my American school located in rural Boulogne before it became a near-suburb city. The school was created in 1946 to serve the children of arriving private sector expats like my parents. It was situated in a country setting on what had been a small farm before the war and a German army barracks during the occupation.

In France, I was a childhood witness to the cold war, NATO, and the Marshall Plan. I became a young participant in a multinational, multicultural society that expats form in their host countries. I would go on to study international relations and comparative government at Yale with ambitions for an international career and life. It pretty much turned out that way.

If any of you have seen a breakthrough television series of some years ago called *Mad Men*, you will know what I am talking about. For those who haven't, let me give you a brief synopsis. This show is about life in the advertising industry in the 1960s. The title evokes Madison Avenue, which was the location and moniker for the industry just as Wall Street brands the financial world. *Mad Men* is essentially an adult evening soap opera, but it was the first to document everyday life in a bygone time as opposed to dramatic historical events. This was its breakthrough. The show ran for seven seasons.

I became a "mad man" in the '60s and worked on Madison Avenue for twenty-five years. For those who know the show, the title enhances its dramatic appeal but in reality the term did not exist. I enjoyed a growing career and was happy in New York when in 1975 at age 32 I made a fateful decision. I joined a summerhouse in the Hamptons

Chapter 4

A Man and a Woman

New York City is unattractive to many in summertime. Those who could afford country houses used them to escape the city on weekends. Many young urban professional singles escaped by joining "group houses" in the Hamptons. These were enormous mansions on big estates. They dated to the 1920s "Great Gatsby" era of F. Scott Fitzgerald on Eastern Long Island with its fabulous beaches. Modern-day owners could no longer keep them up without renting them to yuppies who shared the costs.

I bought a half share in a ten-bedroom house run by city friends. This meant I could go there every other weekend. Cissie joined the same house, having made the same fateful decision the same year. But her half share was for the other weekends, so we could have never met. However, in mid-July the gods smiled again. Cissie's flight schedule forced her to trade weekends with another member and we found ourselves there at the same time.

Around midafternoon that Saturday, I came back from the beach or a tennis game and did what 32-year-olds do. I poured myself a cocktail, picked up a folding beach chair, put in into the shallow end of the pool, and sat in it up to my neck in water with the cocktail held on high. It was a beautiful day and no one was around. All of a sudden the side door in the mansion opened and an incredibly beautiful blond girl in a white lace-like bikini appeared. I took one look at her and thought, *forget it—you can't afford her.* A girl who looked like her was probably invited out to the best restaurants and clubs in NYC. "Out of my league" and I only had a VW Beetle in the driveway.

Cissie came over to the side of the pool, wondering who was this idiot sitting in the pool in a deck chair. She said, "I'm Cissie Ekvall, what are you doing?"

I replied, "I'm Peter Barnet, nice to meet you, I'm just sitting here on a hot day enjoying a cocktail. I know it looks a bit bizarre but I'm not."

So we chatted for a bit and established that Cissie was Swedish and a Pan Am stewardess. She had just come back from a layover in Saint Tropez where she bought the bikini. Now I was certain I could not afford her.

I told her I was an account supervisor in an ad agency working on the Procter & Gamble account. She asked what brands I advertised and I told her: Bounty Paper Towels and White Cloud Toilet Paper.

She reacted, "Toilet paper, is that interesting?"

So, says me digging the hole deeper, "Actually it's the softest toilet paper on earth."

She asked, "Do you use it?"

I answered, "Every day." And with that I knew I was never going to get out of the gate.

Cissie smiled and walked away.

But I was wrong. I would get out of the gate and it would begin that weekend.

We found ourselves on the Saturday night dinner squad. Every member of the house had to participate once a summer in cooking dinner for the house on Saturday night. The house organizer detailed Cissie and me to do the shopping for it and gave us a list of items to buy at the supermarket. They were for thirty people expected that evening. So, we bought the stuff and helped cook it up, etc. all the time chatting away and getting to know each other.

Cissie asked me for a ride back into the city Sunday afternoon. We were four in my VW with Cissie in the back seat sitting behind me. Again, we chatted away and when I dropped her off I knew my first impressions had been paranoid. I could afford her on my junior exec means.

Lightening struck in September. It was the last weekend and all house members were going out to the house. But a bad storm descended on the city on Friday noontime and driving to the Hamptons in it was impossible. So I called the other members and offered a party at my new apartment on 57th st in Manhattan. I spent the afternoon shopping for food and wine. The party was called for 7:00 pm and despite the awful weather pretty much everyone came.

Cissie arrived first at 7:00 sharp, a good twenty minutes before the others started trickling in. Her punctual arrival was my initial introduction to Swedish social culture. Swedes arrive on time. It is considered rude to come late, unlike in the US where arriving at the exact minute would be unrefined. I opened the front door and remember that moment still.

Cissie was dressed in a light green summer evening dress. Everything about her was elegant and breathtaking. She smiled and tilted her head in a charming way and said, "Good evening, Peter. How nice of you to do this tonight. I hope I'm not too early."

I said, "Of course not," but it was obvious I was not fully ready for the party.

Cissie offered to help set up the bar. (This was my first co-op apartment and I had turned its tiny dining room into a stand behind bar with three stools. I thought that would be far more entertaining than a dinner table and chairs.) Cissie looked at it a bit critically, I thought.

People arrived, the wine flowed, the food disappeared, and the conversations hummed. I played the host, making certain glasses were full. As I cruised around, I noticed Cissie talking with someone across the room. I heard her say, "He's not in the same league as Peter Barnet."

My antenna swiveled immediately to that incoming signal and it remained in my receiver for the rest of the evening. Had I heard right? Did she really say that?

Folks started to leave. The weather forecast predicted clearing skies and good weather for the morning. People wanted to get out to the Hamptons early for this final weekend of the summer. Cissie and another man were the last to leave. He was a gracious confirmed bachelor and had offered to take her home. I said good night to them as they moved into the hall and then reached out to stop Cissie.

She turned and I said, "Would you mind helping me cleanup a bit?"

She smiled, thanked the confirmed bachelor for his kind offer to squire her home, and came back into the apartment. We cleaned the place up and then sat down on the living room couch for a nightcap. It was late—around 1:00 am. We sat on that couch all night talking and falling in love. I took her home at 5:00 am and we agreed I would pick her up in my Beetle at noon. It would be our first and last weekend in the Hamptons house in love.

We were now an "item" and saw each other whenever we were both in town between her flights for Pan Am and my weekly commute to Cincinnati for my job.

...

Paris, April 2018

Claude Lelouche's "A Man and a Woman" was re-released in France and played at our local theater in Passy to our utter delight. They handed out a special flyer that told the story of how Lelouche had created the film in 1966. He wrote the original screenplay in three weeks after observing a man and a woman walking on the beach at Deauville, Normandy. It's about two widowed young people: the man is a racecar driver whose wife has died of cancer, the woman has lost her husband, a dashing stunt man in the movies, to an accident on set. They each have one child whom they have placed in a boarding school in Deauville. They meet visiting their children at the school and take them for a walk on the beach.

They are still grieving and conflicted but start to connect. Their budding romance helps them live again. The story is set to incredible Brazilian music, and told with charming outings with the kids, movie stunt flashbacks, race car driving scenes, and the man's dramatic drive across France in a Mustang to see the woman again in Deauville and profess his love for her. The film made Lelouche a star director.

We went to an afternoon screening and I read the flyer to Cissie before the film began. Her reactions were subdued but I knew she was enjoying the story and the film with its Brazilian music. After all, this was our movie and our song. We held hands during most of the film and talked about it afterwards. Cissie's disease did not affect her long-term memory so she remembered it and enjoyed the memory. This was a good day for us both.

My memories of our romance and youth, my proposal and Cissie's acceptance, all came flooding back. But I knew we could not relive those days. My feelings of loss and forever lost overwhelmed me inside but I kept myself together on the outside. It was important to continue our "good day."

I cooked Cissie's favorite dinner, salmon with boiled dill potatoes, and opened a good bottle of white wine. She went to bed afterwards, as she had missed her afternoon nap. This was a good day for my wife in her shrinking world, yes, indeed.

...

New York, November 1975

On a chilly Sunday afternoon in November 1975, we went back to my apartment after first seeing "A Man and a Woman" at the Paris theater. It featured foreign films. I did the only thing I could do after seeing such a romantic French film. I asked Cissie to marry me...and she said yes, but not now.

"Why not now?" I blurted.

She replied, "I have always thought weddings should be in June and in beautiful weather, so I want a June wedding with my mother here. That's why."

I said, "OK, I can understand that, and if the wait doesn't kill me, it's a deal."

Christmas was upon us. Cissie celebrated it on Christmas Eve, the Swedish custom, unlike Americans who celebrate on Christmas Day. Cissie lived with another Swedish stewardess who was also engaged and to a fun Greek guy who worked in a Greek nightclub on the West Side. (He would later become a successful restaurateur.)

The girls invited their two non-Swede fiancées to their apartment for the traditional Swedish Jule smorgasbord. It was fabulous. It was also my first experience with aquavit and the Swedish custom of "down the hatch" toasting. Oh boy! Over the years Cissie would insist on having family and friends for the Jule smorgasbord with as many as twenty dishes. She made them all over three days before the 24th...with one exception: I made the meatballs.

On Christmas day we went to my parents for dinner and announced our engagement to them. It was quite a couple of days.

Cissie stayed at my apartment from then on. I had a king size bed but it seemed we were rarely in it at the same time. I slept by night and worked by day; Cissie slept by day and worked by night. The only time I saw her in her baby blue iconic uniform was when she left for the airport or came in from a flight. God, she looked cute.

Once when we were actually together I came home from the office, heard noises, and saw shadows in the kitchen as two men from the building's staff struggled to move my beloved bar out the back door. Cissie was in the kitchen directing them.

"What are you doing? "I asked with a raised voice more out of surprise than anger.

Cissie replied, "I hate that thing and it's in terrible shape."

She had a point about its condition. One leg was propped up by *La Petite Larousse* dictionary.

After some conversation, the men put the bar back and left. I poured Cissie a drink and we sat down at the bar. This was a sensitive moment.

So I said to her, "This might be a cultural thing but we have an expression in America. It goes like this: marry the man today and change his ways tomorrow. Isn't this a little premature? I agree it has to go but could we let me keep it awhile longer and dump it as part of a larger redecorating?"

Cissie laughed and agreed but had made her point. The bar's days were numbered.

Cissie would reveal herself to be a brilliant interior decorator and hostess. Our homes would be a subject of joy for us and admiration by friends.

...

Paris, May 2018

"I know we are only six but don't you think it would be nicer in the living room than in the dining room?" I asked.

"I don't care. You decide," Cissie replied after a bit.

"I think the dining room table in the living room is more elegant and comfortable. It's a bit more work but I think it's a good idea, and don't worry. I'm cooking. You don't have to do anything."

"Good," she said.

"I think we'll start with white asparagus and then have coquelets with dill potatoes. I've bought apple tarts for dessert, no cheese. It's simpler."

"Good," she said after a bit.

Cissie was famous for her dinner parties amongst our friends in Paris. The big decisions were in which dining room to have them and of course to select the menu. We normally entertained for six in the dining room next to the kitchen. For larger groups we had to use the table in the living room. This time I thought the living room would be more appropriate because the conversation would be of substance, as we were all interested in current events and even writing about them. Somehow, I reasoned that a less intimate and "grander setting" would enhance the discussions. Such was life in an "apartement de reception." But now I was planning the menu and doing the cooking.

Our guests did not yet know about Cissie's growing problem. Few would have noticed as the disease hides pretty well in the earlier years. Cissie conversed just fine but she talked a lot less than before. However, that doesn't necessarily signal anything but her current mood to most visitors.

It was a lovely evening. The two ladies congratulated me on my cooking. "Cissie, you have trained him well", they quipped.

Everyone remarked on the beauty of the apartment and Cissie's taste in furnishings. She was gracious but not loquacious. The apartment was all Cissie and now its joys were slowly slipping away from her.

...

Riverside, June 1976

Cissie and I married on a glorious day at my parent's house in Connecticut. A Lutheran minister performed the ceremony. He was, by chance, a second generation Swede. He had insisted on meeting us a few weeks before the wedding and we had agreed to come to his church in Stamford on a Sunday, an hour train ride from the city. We had been out with Cissie's roommate and her fiancée at his nightclub, drinking ouzo and dancing on tables until about 4:00 am on the Saturday night before our meeting with the minister.

After Sunday services we met. He took one look at us (not a pretty sight) and he lectured us about his concerns with youth and drinking. We were too wiped out to argue.

Our plan was to marry at 4:30 pm in front of the fireplace mantle in the house and then go out side to the terrace for the reception and dînatoire. We had invited about fifty guests. It is customary for the minister and his wife to join the reception for a glass of champaign and then leave after thirty minutes or an hour or so. We had hired a three-piece combo to play music on the terrace. Three hours later, the pastor was chasing my mother around the pool and his wife was leading the band. Both were gassed. You can't make this stuff up.

A little later, I slipped on the flagstones in my new dress shoes and came down hard on the outside of my right foot. I knew it was hurt. When our guests had left, we drove back into the city in the Beetle, and when we arrived to the apartment, I could barely get out of the car. We got upstairs. Cissie laid me on the bed and took off my sock. The foot was black.

She said with confidence, "I can fix this."

She went into the kitchen and came back with a bottle of vinegar, a hand towel, the Sunday NY Times, a ball of string, and a pair of scissors. Ten minutes later, I looked like an amputee in a hospital. I was flat on my back with all this stuff wrapped and tied around the foot and couldn't move...and my foot hurt like hell. *And this was my wedding night! And we were flying to Nice the next night for our honeymoon!* I felt like a compete jerk.

Cissie told me this was her mother's cure for stuff like this. I did feel a little better by morning but the foot looked terrible and I feared it might be broken.

So somehow I got dressed and got myself to the nearby emergency room at Roosevelt Hospital. The day before had featured a major annual parade in NYC that came with a lot of celebrating by the attendees. The emergency room on that Sunday morning looked like a war zone.

I sat there feeling miserable, the only person not wounded by someone else, when a voice called out, "Barnet, get your ass in here!"

I looked up and there was a classmate I had not seen since graduation. He was the doctor on duty that morning. We exchanged good-natured insults: "Yes, I had always been an asshole." But he really saved my day. I left an hour later with an ace bandage around the foot (it was not broken) and a certificate to give to Pan Am for a more comfortable seat. When I got home, Cissie was just getting up. We were both relieved.

We arrived in Nice and drove to Eze Village, a mountain town with breathtaking views of the Mediterranean. The hotel was on top, about one hundred steps above the parking to the entrance. So Cissie left me in the car and climbed/ran up to reception.

She blurted out, "Hi, I'm Cissie Ekvall, oops Barnet I mean. I just got married in New York and we're here on our honeymoon. My husband can't walk. Could you send someone to help him?"

After a time, two guys with a cart came down to the car and when they saw me inside they looked relieved. I'm sure they had seen this before. A young beauty just married an older rich American who won't last long and leave her a lot of money. He might even die in the saddle at the hotel. Clearly this was not our scenario.

We had a great honeymoon. I was fit to dance in four days and we danced up a storm in Saint Tropez and elsewhere. Real life is often more bizarre than fiction.

You can't make this stuff up.

Our wedding song was "A Man and a Woman."

Peter Barnet

Chapter 5

Munich

We settled into married life in New York in late June. Cissie intended to fly a bit longer and start looking for a banking job in September. I resumed my weekly commute to Cincinnati. But the gods had other plans.

Out of the blue, the agency asked me to represent the firm at a new joint venture with a local agency in Munich. My agency had placed two US clients there and they needed looking after. It was all part of the globalization process and I would be the first American to go overseas. They picked me because I was due reassignment soon and they knew I had lived abroad as a child and just married a European girl who spoke perfect German. I was an ideal match for their needs.

Cissie loved Germany and we decided to do it. She took a leave of absence from Pan Am. We were there for two years and took well to international life. Expat packages were generous in those days so we lived well. We even bought a little sports car, a Triumph Spitfire, and our first dog, a Tsi Tzu. Cissie turned heads driving around Munich with her little dog in the sports car. She referred to it as her Spitzy and named the dog Wuffy. "Cissie and Wuffy in the Spitzy." You can't make this stuff up.

We loved Munich and enjoyed the city. One of our favorite places was a restaurant called Haxn Bauer. It specialized in Bavarian pork joints roasted on a rotisserie. Frau Bauer was a rotund, jovial sixtyish lady who greeted her guests with great warmth. We loved it so that we went once a week with Wuffy. After about a year and fifty-two swinehaxns, Frau Bauer greeted us one evening with a broad smile. Her chef was standing next to her beaming.

She announced that this was a special occasion. Our loyalty had earned us a stamtisch. This is a regular table for patrons who dine a lot in a German restaurant. It was an honor to get one. She identified an excellent table for us going forward and then proceeded to present Cissie with a silver medal, the "Order of the Haxn," and pinned it on her dress. Not done, she pulled a haxn bone out of her apron and presented it to Wuffy. It is little moments like this that add to the charm of life. We never forgot it.

We returned to the states with many memories and adventures with Wuffy in the Spitzy. We toured Bavaria, Austria, and Italy and got as far as Venice in that little car. Business took me to Berlin, Frankfurt, Dusseldorf, Paris, and London. Cissie often came along and she introduced me to Sweden and Denmark. I met her old boyfriend in Gothenburg, who was married with a first child on the way. We became friends. Cissie's mother was with us a lot and most welcome. She spoke enough English to get by and communicate with me. We became close.

Cissie resigned from Pan Am in the spring of 1977. They had activated her, but to fly out of New York whilst living in Munich made no sense. She also had secured a marketing research job at Timex Watches and enjoyed it.

However, there was another reason. Cissie had developed rheumatoid arthritis a year before we married. There is nothing worse for it than stewardess life with constant changes in altitude pressures and serving passengers from heavy trays, etc. Her stewardess days were over.

I guess the gods like to balance things so if they are too good, they have to give something bad. This one was real bad. Rheumatoid arthritis attacks women primarily. It appears in their early thirties and often disappears in their early sixties. In between it causes major suffering and damage to joints. And this is how it went with Cissie. The disease compromised her ability to play tennis and ski. Her hands would swell whenever she used them strenuously. She loved to garden but gardening did not love her. By the time her arthritis disappeared at age 63, Cissie's hands looked more like claws. Her finger joints were destroyed.

Cissie was stoic about her arthritis. She bore the pain and was determined to lead a normal life. But it was not easy and sometimes it overwhelmed her. I admired her courage and on our doctor's advice pushed her to carry on.

Cissie on the Terrace in Munich, 1977

Peter Barnet

Chapter 6

The Big Apple Years

We lived in Manhattan on east 57th Street from our return in June 1978 until summer 1992. Cissie went to work at Kosta Boda, a Scandinavian crystal company, and I continued at the agency and traveled both at home and abroad.

In 1979, we built a small country house in the Hamptons near our old group summerhouse, and in September 1980, our son Christopher was born.

In 1982, I left the agency to join another one in a great job.

Cissie exercised a long interest in Chinese art (that began in Bangkok) by working two days a week at Christies, the auction house, in its "oriental" department. She had stopped working when our son was born.

She called me at the office around noon on her first day. "Peter, I've just seen a Chinese charger. It's fabulous. It was sold to a dealer but she returned it. The reserve is only $1500. They are having a big argument about whether it is nineteenth century or Ming. I think it is Ming. My boss is willing to give it to me for the reserve price. I want to buy it. It is fabulous and an incredible opportunity. You will love it. What do you think?"

I asked, "What's a charger?"

"It's a big bowl. It's blue and white and has a double-headed eagle design. I just know it is Ming Dynasty."

"Exactly when was the Ming Dynasty?" I queried.

"Late fifteenth to eighteenth centuries," she replied. "I just know it is a Ming!"

"Cissie," I said. "Christies is paying you $15 a day and the bowl is $1500, and it's only your first day. I can't work hard enough to keep up with you if you are going to do this every day. We would have to sell the apartment."

There was a long silence and then Cissie said in serious tone, "Peter, I know this is a Ming. And if I'm right, it's worth a fortune. And I absolutely love it! I'll buy it with my own money."

So she did and she was right. It was a Ming; it was fabulous!

Cissie would become an accomplished expert in Chinese porcelain and make some very clever purchases when she saw value that even Christie's did not. She went back to school at Columbia University to pursue a master's degree in Chinese Art. The A student was back! She researched and wrote her thesis on the bowl.

Her prized charger dated to 1530 in Macao. It was part of an alter set used my monks at the Saint Augustine Monastery. The double-headed eagle that she thought might have been the Romanoff cote of arms was actually that of the Saint Augustine's, a Portuguese order. They established their mission in Macao in the late 15th Century. Cissie corresponded with the head of the order in Portugal to establish the Charger's authenticity and a highly reputed London dealer confirmed that it was both rare and real. It was worth "a fortune".

In 1983, we bought a larger apartment in the same building on 57th Street. Cissie refused decorating help from a lady friend of my mother's and did it all herself. She was brilliant with a great eye for style and a concept mixing Chinese, Japanese, Italian modern and French 18th Century pieces. She extended her fashion philosophy of a few good items as opposed to a lot of so so stuff to furnishings. The apartment was spectacular. The bar was long gone and wasn't missed.

For the next several years we prospered in our lifestyle. We enjoyed the city during the week and the Hamptons on weekends. Cissie would stay out there all summer with Chris, who went to day camp and I would come out on weekends and for vacation. I bought a fishing boat but proved to be one terrible fisherman. Chris and a friend were so excited to catch a fish initially but by the time they were six they had lost interest. That pretty much illustrates how bad I was at fishing.

Hampton's social life centered on dinner parties. Cissie and I hosted our share. She had become a marvelous cook and we would alternate between creative dinners and barbecues.

...

Paris, November 2018

I went to my book group and told Cissie I would be home by 7:00 to cook us dinner. I knew she would nap until then. When I came home she was in the kitchen.

"Peter," she said, "I wanted to make you dinner tonight. It's almost ready."

"Cissie," I replied, "this is so sweet of you! Give me a hug!"

I gave her a big smile but inside, I was horrified. The handle of the big frying pan was sticking out of the oven with the heat on and the door open. The vegetables were in a saucepan on the stove in their wrappers and more. Had I been five minutes later, it could have been a disaster. But I thanked her profusely.

Looking back, I think this was one of my saddest moments during Cissie's decent.

...

West Hampton, August 1982

Cissie decided to make Peking duck for twelve people. She had never tried this before. She bought three Long Island ducks (which were very famous before the duck farms gave way to country houses). To get the skin right she hung the ducks in the basement for one day with a hairdryer on them and then hung them from three terrace lights outdoors. Anyone who saw them would have thought that these ducks had been executed and hung there as an example and warning to other ducks. They were delicious!

In 1989, I switched agencies again and began to commute weekly to Los Angeles.

I had little international travel except for vacations and visiting Cissie's mother in Gothenburg. Chris loved going there because the city has a great amusement park and he loved his grandmother.

In 1990, the gods became mischievous. My new agency asked me to move to LA. My client was there and transcontinental commuting made little sense on a host of measures. At the same time a client from my first agency who I had worked with in Munich became a new business prospect for my new agency. They offered me a choice of moving to LA or staying in New York to pitch the new prospect and lead it if we won. Cissie and I decided to stay and this turned out to be a life changing decision.

We all know there can be turning points in life. There usually are. It is also true that we rarely recognize a turning point when it occurs. We need time and perspective to see it. Had we decided to go to Los Angeles much of the rest of our story would have been different. But we stayed in New York, won that client, and two years later we moved to Paris with it. Twenty-eight years later, we are still in Paris.

Chapter 7

Le Vesinet

Paris, July 1992

We rented a house in the Paris suburbs in the town of Le Vesinet, a glorious place just below Saint Germain en Laye, a small city with a royal chateau that had served as the summer residence of French Kings until Louis XIV decided to move and build the much grander and world famous Versailles.

The house dated to the 1860s. Le Vesinet had been split off from the royal grounds of Saint Germain en Laye when the first train line from Paris reached St. Germain. Napoleon III had made that decision and created Le Vesinet as a country/weekend setting for his friends at court and the bourgeoisie. He had built canals and parks with wonderful nature walks and the homes built at that time like ours were distinctive and lovely. And Le Vesinet was only twenty minutes from Paris on today's trains. Cissie and I thought we had gone to heaven.

Chris went to school in the neighborhood and could bike there every day. He would become bilingual in French. I commuted to Paris on the train. Cissie met neighbors and other expatriot families who also favored Le Vesinet. And there were a few Swedish ladies married to Frenchmen living there. We both fell in love with the town and made friends quickly.

A French couple that lived behind us on the park came over one night and asked if we knew about our house. It had two bedrooms upstairs: a big one with a sleeping area and a one step up boudoir. It featured a bathtub surrounded by 19th century paintings of cherubs at play. They also decorated the space above the doors through out the house.

Cissie and I thought this was so charming and mused that this was how some French lived in the 1860s with the bathtub in the bedroom. After all, it was a period when plumbing was new, if it existed at all. We were wrong.

Our neighbors told us that we had rented what was originally a "maison cocotte."

We looked uncomprehending so they explained that this was a house built by a rich man for his mistress. A maison cocotte was a mistress house. He had his family home in Paris with his wife and children and a country place for his mistress. That explained the cherubs frolicking over the bathtub and doors. I reasoned the smaller second bedroom was for him when his mistress was upset about something and exiled him to it. How cool was this.

Cissie directed our move into the house with the furniture from our New York apartment. We installed an IKEA kitchen and Cissie wallpapered the dining room that gave onto the garden and the breakfast room off the kitchen. It was sublime. The property was lavish with an enormous beach tree anchoring the garden and a magnificent blue spruce along the driveway. The yard was fenced with hedges facing the park on one side of the house and a with a simple wire fence alone on the other side along the driveway. It separated the property from the next-door neighbor. One entered from the street through a solid metal gate.

I learned early in our marriage that telling Cissie what to do was a useless exercise (remember the bar). Her independent spirit was an asset but at times it could get her into trouble.

In November 1992, our new company car arrived. It was a BMW 5 series and tres snappy. Cissie and I were excited. (We were excited about everything that year.) On that particular day, Cissie was in Gothenburg visiting her mother who at 85 was weakening. She was due back the following morning and I was leaving at dawn for a day trip to the British Midlands.

Chris and I picked up the new car at the BMW dealer after he came home from school that afternoon. It was equipped with a child-safety-door-locking system that was new to me and a bit tricky. I showed Chris how it worked. I left both sets of keys in the bedroom and called Cissie. I told her the new car had arrived but asked her not to drive it until I returned or not before Chris could show her how to work the door locking system. He would be home by 4:00 pm and I would get back late.

The next day our meetings in the Midlands ended early so three of us drove to the airport to catch an earlier flight. I was driving. One of us had an early model cell phone so I asked him if I could use it to call my wife to alert her that I would be home for dinner after all.

So I called home; a Frenchman answered.

I asked, "Who are you?"

He answered, "I am your neighbor."

I asked, "Where are you?"

He answered, "I am in your bedroom."

My colleagues in the car heard this exchange and cracked up.

I asked, "What are you doing in my bedroom?"

He answered, "I am looking for your car keys. Madame is locked in your new car. She told me to look for the spare keys here."

Now my colleagues were laughing hysterically.

I asked him how long my wife had been trapped in the car. He said quite some time. He had come home for lunch around noon. She was in the car. He had never met her but she waved vigorously to him and he waved back. He thought that was very nice. But when he came out at 2:00 pm she was still in the car and started waving desperately to him and seemed to be shouting at him, too. He realized then that something was wrong so he climbed over the wire fence and tried to open the car door. He could hear her now. He was searching our bedroom for the spare keys when I called. My colleagues collapsed in hysterical laughter and frankly so did I. The Frenchman found the keys and freed Cissie from the new BMW. She was understandably not amused.

When I got home. Cissie told her side of the story. "Stop laughing! This wasn't funny! God, what a day! I arrived around eleven this morning and when I came through the gate, there was the BMW, all new, navy blue with the tan interior. It was so elegant looking. I couldn't believe we had a BMW! I went upstairs to unpack and saw the two keys on the bureau and came back down to the kitchen to fix some lunch. I looked out at the BMW again. I just couldn't concentrate on lunch. I went out to the driveway and looked all around it and said to myself: Chris won't be home until three. I don't dare drive it but there can't be anything wrong with just sitting in it. So I went back upstairs and got the key, came back, unlocked the BMW (it was so exciting, a BMW!) and got in. I love the smell of new leather.

"After a few minutes, I thought it couldn't do any harm to start the engine; I won't put it in gear. So I turned the car on and let it run for a few minutes, you know, just to get familiar with everything, and when I turned it off, all of a sudden all the doors and windows closed and locked and I couldn't figure out how to open the door.

"Stop laughing! This isn't funny! I was stuck in there for hours! Thank God that nice man next door finally understood I was trapped and got me out. I could have been in there until Chris came home. And you, stop laughing, too, Chris! This isn't funny!"

Of course, it wasn't funny to Cissie but it was to us.

The following morning was Saturday. I saw my neighbor in his yard and went over to the wire fence to introduce myself, and thanked him again for rescuing my wife. He was laughing in wonder about it, too. We chatted a bit and made male jokes about our spouses, all in good humor. He thought Cissie's adventure had been incredible.

Two weeks later, Cissie came home from shopping and when she went to open the gate (it was not on a remote control) she realized she had left her keys in the house. There was no way to get in until Chris came home from school with his key. So she decided to climb over the gate, which was quite high.

She got back into the BMW and pushed its nose up to the gate so she could climb onto the hood and then the gate. She got to the top of it, put one leg over to the inside and froze. She looked like a weather vane on top of it. Just as she froze in fear on top of the gate, the neighbor drove out of his next door with his wife and as they slowly passed our gate with Cissie on top, they looked at her with dropped jaws and disbelief. I figured they must have dined out regularly after that telling their friends about the crazy Swedish woman who lived next door. You can't make this stuff up.

Oh, Cissie did succeed getting over the gate and into the yard. The house was open so she got her keys and opened the gate. But she never tried that again.

I tell you this story, not to make fun of her, but to illustrate the adventurous spirit of my beautiful and brilliant wife. No one ever thought she was dull. Au contraire!

Chapter 8

Ritz Escoffier Ecole de Cuisine

In 1994, the gods turned nasty. They do this sometimes.

Business difficulties forced us to give up our beloved Le Vesinet and maison cocotte. We returned to the US. Chris went off to a reputed junior boarding school in Western Massachusetts that had its own small mountain and a ski team. We had raised Chris from age 2 to ski and he joined the school's team.

He skied for three hours a day over two winter seasons there and became a top skier.

I went to work for a Mexican multinational competitor to my employer in Paris. I would be away a lot traveling in the US and Latin America.

Cissie decided to return to France and accomplish another life ambition. She enrolled in a three-month cooking course at France's famous Ritz Escoffier Ecole de Cuisine. It was located in the Ritz Hotel at Place Vendome in central Paris. She rented a small, furnished one bedroom apartment in Montmartre just below Sacre Coeur. It was charming and not expensive but quite a commute on the Metro to the Ritz. She would return to the US just before Christmas.

Ritz Escoffier attracted some older people, interested in improving their cooking skills as an avocation. However, the role of the school was professional training for young men and women pursuing careers as restaurateurs and caterers, etc.

Much has been written about the tyranny in the kitchen of head chefs. They are in a creative and disciplined profession with perfectionist high standards. Their business depends on it. The Ritz school was training future head chefs in top restaurants. As such the school's professors resembled drill instructors in elite military services.

Cissie was a little overwhelmed at first, but A students apply themselves and she was determined to excel. Her class included some interesting classmates. One young woman was a captain in the Israeli army who had seen combat and was preparing for a professional cooking career.

Another was an American opera singer who was there for fun. Two months into the course she challenged classmates to bet on whether she could hit a high note strong enough to collapse a soufflé as it came out of the oven. She could, and whenever she got fed up with the seriousness of the course she would go on a soufflé-popping rampage in the basement kitchen. Diners in the elegant Ritz dining room above could hear her aria and wonder what the devil was going on.

You can't make this stuff up.

There were several old widows in Cissie's building in Montmartre, which did not have an elevator. Cissie got to know them a bit and would bring them pastries from her baking class. She would let them know when and they would get together in one apartment to have coffee and wait for Cissie to arrive with the goodies. She had to haul them up to the third or fourth floors and was always greeted with smiles of anticipation. Cissie became a popular and very welcome neighbor for these widows.

Toward the end of the course, Cissie had to learn how to cut meat and filet fish across a range of dishes. Some of these exercises were assigned as homework. Her local butcher must have found her interesting. One evening she had to prepare and cook a rack of veal. The butcher asked how many chops she wanted and she said six, please.

He remarked, "You must be having a big dinner party tonight."

Cissie answered, "No, it's just for me."

He was dumbfounded.

Cissie graduated in December. The final exam required her to cook a three-course meal designated by the school and to present it to a panel of judges. They would taste and rate each dish and if she passed on each course she would receive her diploma. She was incredibly nervous but came through another A for Cissie.

Cissie came home to Christmas in the Hamptons. Chris was back from school and we were excited to see her. I asked her what she was going to cook for Christmas dinner given all she had learned.

Her response was, "Nothing. You can do the cooking. I'm cooked out. I think I may give it up."

Chris and I were incredulous. He said, "Oh come on, Mom. You have to cook Christmas dinner. Let's do the smorgasbord."

"Much too much work," Cissie replied.

I got exercised. "What do you mean? You can't be serious. You are going to give up cooking after going to Ritz Escoffier for three months? You know how much this thing cost? You're not serious."

She was serious, sort of, but later rethought that because it seemed unfair to her boys. We were relieved.

Peter Barnet

Chapter 9

Exile, 1995, and Escape

This period was difficult for family life. Chris returned to junior boarding school and I was travelling up to six days a week. Cissie was alone in our country house most of the time. We had rented out our apartment when we left for France and the tenants had a lease with one more year. There are only two words to describe life alone in the Hamptons in winter: "lonely" and "boring" and this is how Cissie understandably felt. Loneliness is a most terrible thing!

The Gods must have heard her lament. In September, I ran into a guy at La Guardia airport who I knew from the advertising business. He had just moved to London in a top management job at a global agency. I told him I knew Europe well and if he ever needed some help over there to give me a call.

Four weeks later, I came home to our summerhouse from a trip around 6:00 pm on a Friday evening. I was scheduled to fly out again on Monday. Cissie greeted me with a smile. I hadn't seen one of those for a while. She told me a man had called from a famous executive search firm, knew I travelled a lot, and insisted I call him back no matter how late on Friday night. Cissie was excited. I think had this been a job opportunity with the NYC Sanitation Department to collect garbage in Manhattan, she would have told me to go for it. She was that desperate and I didn't blame her. I called him.

The headhunter (as the executive search guys are called) told me he was looking for a senior advertising man for a top job in Europe with the agency my friend at La Guardia had joined. The job was worldwide but based in Paris and my friend had recommended me to the search firm. He told me a bit about the job. The fit was obvious. I agreed to meet him in New York later the following week after my scheduled trip on Monday to Mexico City.

When I hung up I told an excited and anxious Cissie a bit about it and that it was based in Paris. Her eyes almost popped out of her head. I was exhausted from an arduous travel week and went into the kitchen to pour myself a drink. I heard the trapdoor to the attic opening and the stars unfolding and by the time I turned around Cissie was coming back down the attic stairs with a suitcase.

"What the devil are you doing, sweetie?" I said.

She answered, "I have to start thinking about what I am going to take to Paris."

I laughed and remarked, "Darling, isn't this a bit premature? That was only the headhunter on the phone. First I have to meet him, then I have to interview with several people at the agency, and then they have to offer me the job. I have to get the job first and I might not get it. Either way, this will take some time."

Cissie smiled. "I know that," she said, "but I also know you are going to get this job because it was made for you and it's in Paris! So I am planning ahead."

I smiled back and said, "Let me pour you a drink."

Chapter 10

Passy

Cissie was prescient. I did get the job. In March 1996 we moved into an apartment in the sixteenth arrondissement in the village of Passy. Paris has twenty arrondissements (or districts) and is further divided by several villages in each. The sixteenth is on the right bank of the Seine River across from the Eiffel Tower. It is an upscale area next to the western suburbs and Boulogne where I had gone to school. My new office was there, too.

We did not return to Le Vesinet, though our hearts were there. Chris had stayed at his boarding school (he had bounced enough) and Cissie did not want to be alone in a house when I was travelling. I was away a lot in this worldwide job. So it seemed sensible to live in the city.

Most corporate expats use a transfer agent funded by their employer to help them find housing and get settled in France. They base their fees on time to research the market, understand their client's objectives, select a list of candidates, and show two–three places.

Cissie had re-rented her Montmartre apartment from Ritz Escoffier days in January. This was preferable to staying in a hotel. We hired the same agent who had found our Maison Cocotte four years earlier. Cissie did not know the city well enough to zero in on a neighborhood straight away. The transfer agent showed her several arrondissements and finally Cissie settled on Passy and an apartment.

By then she had seen seventeen apartments and the transfer agent was talking to herself (maybe raving to herself is a more accurate description). But Cissie knew what she wanted and what

I would like and critically she knew the space that would go ideally with our furniture. She drove the transfer lady nuts but she got it right. So we rented it and moved in.

Moving is always challenging and this one was a bit complex because our furniture in Le Vesinet that had come from our apartment in New York had to go into storage upon our return to the states as our apartment was rented. So it came out of storage for the transatlantic return voyage to France. We threw in a few pieces from our country house that the movers packed and added to the shipment.

I went into West Hampton that morning to buy fixings for lunch. They were in a brown paper bag and I put it on the kitchen counter when I returned home. Things were so hectic that morning that I completely forgot about it.

Six weeks later the movers in Passy unpacked our stuff and there was the brown paper bag. Picture what ham, lettuce, tomato, and two rolls would look like after six weeks in a shipping container. But I guess we were lucky that those bozos in West Hampton hadn't packed our dog, too. Actually I believe we would have noticed that.

Passy is a family-oriented community with some of the best schools in Paris. It has a main shopping street that is lively with chic boutiques, food stores, and all the necessities of life. It has a modern shopping mall with a supermarket next to traditional markets that are wonderful. It is a movable feast.

The village has a history of note for Americans because it was here that Benjamin Franklin lived and held his offices in 1777 when he was the Continental Congress' minister to the Court of Louis XVI. In fact, he lived on our street. In Franklin's time, Passy was open vineyards, a chateau and some palace-like structures. These gave way to Haussmannian apartment buildings in the 1900–1920 period that add so much to the beauty of Paris.

The apartment was Cissie's triumph. Realtors characterized it as an "apartement de reception." Our New York furnishings fit into it divinely. Cissie added some new antique pieces and art. It was gracious, even spectacular, but livable at the same time. It neither looked like it had been "decorated" nor like a museum with velvet ropes guarding the rooms. It was comfortable, natural, and "real." We installed the IKEA kitchen from Le Vesinet. We entertained a lot and cooked up a storm for friends. We loved the apartment and our lives.

In 2005, we bought the apartment. The building was co-oped and we were the first to buy. Over the next few years we put in a new kitchen renovated the bathrooms, installed a made-to-measure closet for our clothes, rewired and modernized the electricity, and painted the walls in mauve with white moldings.

Now it was 100% Cissie's creations.

There is a ladies magazine in Sweden called *Damen*. They frequently do features on the lifestyle of Swedish ladies abroad. Someone suggested they do one on Cissie and our apartment. She accepted and when it was published, Cissie received emails from friends all over the world.

In 2001, I retired after thirty-six years in the advertising business. Chris was now at the University of Denver and doing a lot of skiing. We saw no reason to return to the US. We had sold both the apartment and country house and begun to vacation in the Stockholm Archipelago each summer. We were happy. We visited Chris in Denver and he came home to Paris for vacations and summers. We were all happy.

A week after I retired, the moving lady at my firm called and started telling me how to arrange out return to the US. She rattled on about three bids from moving companies, timing and planning the move, and more. She went on and on and finally I interrupted and said, "I do not believe all this is necessary at this time. Maybe we will need this help in the future, but not now."

There was a long silence on the other end and finally her voice came back and she asked in an uncertain, incredulous tone, "You mean you are not coming back?"

I answered, "Yes, that's about it...at least not at this time."

She was nonplussed and went on, "I have never lost an expat before. All my expats come home. How do I handle this? Your contract pays your way home. Are you sure you want to do this?"

I told her not to worry. We never spoke again but I expect she shared this unprecedented event with her colleagues in the travel department.

In January 2002, Chris took a junior spring semester abroad at The American University of Paris. Cissie and I attended an orientation evening for parents a week before classes began. I had met the university president before and had asked him about the possibilities of teaching a communications course after I retired. He was polite but evasive. He was at the orientation so I took the opportunity to ask him again. Again he was evasive.

A few days later, the phone rang and Cissie answered it. I was in another room on my computer.

She came running in and somewhat nervously told me, "There's a man on the phone from AUP; he sounds high up. He doesn't want to talk to Chris and he doesn't want to talk to me. He only wants to talk to you."

I said, "OK. But don't worry, classes don't begin until next week; Chris can't be in trouble yet."

It was the chairman of the Communications Department. He was going on sabbatical and had hired an outside person to teach his course. The man bailed out at the last minute. The university president had mentioned my name as someone who might be both qualified and available. We agreed to meet on the coming Monday.

It was sheer serendipity. I would teach at AUP for fourteen years and eventually join the faculty full time. Cissie would tell friends that we took Christopher to the orientation, he stayed for one semester, and Peter stayed for many years.

Cissie built a full life in Paris between the Swedish community, a regular Franco-American conversation group with interesting participants, and the Paris chapter of World Wings International, the Alumni Club for Pan Am flight attendants. She devoured Paris cultural life, joining both American and British art and touring groups. She lived in museums and we went to operas and concerts semiregularly.

Cissie became a mainstay at the Swedish Club. Le Circle Suedoise was established around 1900 on rue Rivoli overlooking the Tuilerie Gardens. This is one of Paris's grand boulevards. One of the founders of the Club was Alfred Nobel. He signed his will that established the Nobel Prize in the club's office. That room is still there as well as the desk upon which he signed it. Today it has many uses and remains a must-see spot for visitors to the club.

The Swedish Club has a vibrant social and events calendar with wonderful jazz every Wednesday evening, piano concerts on other nights, art clubs, and lectures from all walks of Swedish life. Many of these events are held in both French and Swedish. Many are in English because the club welcomes international visitors at its activities. The Swedish Ambassador and top government officials have all spoken there. One evening Cissie and I attended a dinner for the crown princess of Sweden. One morning we attended a breakfast for the then–prime minister.

Expatriate clubs all do these kinds of things but few have their own venue...and that makes the Swedish Club special. Cissie attended evenings at least once a week and I was there occasionally as well. We loved the jazz evenings with friends.

Peter Barnet

Chapter 11

Trick or Treat

On October 31, 2013, Cissie and I were at home. It was a Friday night and we had invited a Swedish couple for dinner. They had arrived from Stockholm that afternoon. Cissie was busy preparing for the dinner and I had set the table in the dining room for four. Our guests were expected at 7:00 pm and they would arrive on the dot in the Swedish manner.

October 31 is Halloween in the United States. The French have dabbled with the occasion including kids dressed up like goblins and witches to go door to door "trick or treating "in the hopes of getting some candy. We had some chocolate but did not expect much traffic. The Gods had planned a trick for us that evening. They scheduled it for 7:30 pm.

Our friends arrived; we seated them in the living room and returned to the kitchen to open the champagne and finalize the hors d'oeuves. It is useful for you to understand the layout of the apartment. The kitchen is next to the entrance with a window that gives onto the interior courtyard. The living room is at the other end down a long foyer. It looks out to the street.

At 7:30, I was opening the champagne and Cissie was putting some bread in the toaster. All of a sudden we heard a pop and half the lights in the kitchen went out. I went immediately to the electrical box in a cabinet by the front door to the kitchen, opened the cabinet and saw a small flame coming from the back of the box. I hit the master switch that killed the electricity throughout the apartment and called for help to the guest in the living room. He came right away. After thirty seconds or so of trying to extinguish the now growing fire, I called emergency 911.

I gave the man on the line my name and address, and described what was happening.

He asked one or two questions and then said, "The fire trucks are on their way and should be there in five minutes. Listen to me very carefully and do as I tell you. Open the kitchen window. Close the kitchen door and get everyone out of the apartment *now.*"

We did as instructed. The fire department arrived as predicted and went to work. Within a few more minutes there were four trucks, two hook and ladders, and two carriers with men and hoses. The street was closed, the sirens wailed, and the firemen evacuated the tenants in the building. Forty minutes later, the fire captain invited me to follow him up to the apartment. Cissie took our friends to the corner café to wait for me there.

The rest of the apartment was untouched except there were black smoke streaks on all the walls. But the kitchen was totally destroyed, all black and burnt with twisted metal and the false ceiling collapsed. The instructions the man had given me on the phone to open the window to the courtyard and close the kitchen door had condemned the kitchen but saved the apartment and all its contents. The fire was sucked out into the courtyard. Later a neighbor who witnessed it told me flames of two meters were shooting out of the window. I could not help marvel at the violence of the fire and the ugliness of what was now our kitchen.

We had dinner with our friends at the café and then went home to pack an overnight bag to spend the night at a neighborhood hotel. Our cat that Cissie adored had hidden under our bed far from the fire but was so traumatized that he would not come out, the poor little guy. So we left him and I got him early the following morning. He was fine.

So was Cissie. She was never one to panic. She was resilient.

We never identified the cause of the fire but suspected it was a short in the electrical box. The fire chief told me that we were extremely lucky it happened when we were in the kitchen. Had it happened when we were asleep, we could have been killed. Had it happened when we were away, it could have destroyed the entire building.

We rented a small two bedroom flat down the street and were temporarily settled there in two weeks. This was incredible luck and helped keep our spirits up. The time at the temporary apartment was just fine. Cissie and I met an American couple that lived in the building part of the year and we became close friends. The ladies really appreciated each other.

We continued with our lives as normally as possible. We entertained our friends at small dinners. The kitchen wasn't great but together we made it work. I continued teaching at AUP and Cissie continued with her clubs, conversation and tour groups. She replaced the kitchen in our apartment identically but with different colors and spent three months searching for a new granite counter top. She adjusted the colors on the walls and drove the head painter batty. But the end result was marvelous. She had taken the time and effort to improve on perfection.

It took eight months to restore the apartment and install the new kitchen. We moved back into it in late June 2014.

However, it was during this time that I first wondered if something was wrong with Cissie. Alzheimer's is long present before symptoms begin to appear. She was her resilient self during the restoration period but that resilience would now begin to evaporate.

Peter Barnet

Chapter 12

Vietnam

By early 2016, I had little doubt that Cissie was developing Alzheimer's. I reasoned that our world was going to shrink so we should travel to interesting places while we still could. Travel was so important to us both.

For example Cissie had arranged a three-week trip to Burma in 2003 with a top Parisian travel agency: Voyagers du Monde. It was her second trip. She had taken a group tour there when I was still working in business and now she wanted to go back to show this amazing country to me. This time would be a private tour with an English speaking guide and beautiful hotels. We would tour the country mostly by car and often over dirt roads for adventurous visits in the countryside, lake regions, and off the beaten paths. This was Cissie's approach ever since her Pan Am days and Asian art and culture was her intellectual passion.

Looking back, we rated this adventure as one the two best vacation travels in our lives together.

Cissie had also been on a French tour to Vietnam and loved it. But I had not been there. So we decided to go in March. Cissie was clear that a second visit for her was just great. I decided to travel in style. This might be our travel swansong.

I booked a private tour beginning in Hanoi at the famous Sofitel Angleterre followed by Ha Long Bay, Hue, Da nang, Ho Chi Min city, and then onto Angkor wat and Siem Reap in Cambodia. We had private guides and great accommodations everywhere. Before we departed, I promoted the trip every day to Cissie. I gave her the itinerary and the very snappy travel literature from our agency. I was convinced this would make Cissie excited and happy. I was wrong.

Ten days before departure, Cissie told me, "I don't want to go. I've already been to Vietnam. It's boring."

"What do you mean, dear?" I replied. "You loved your trip to Vietnam and wanted to show it to me. We are going to all the great places and this time we are staying in the best hotels and we'll have private English speaking guides. We were really looking forward to going. And I won't get our money back. It cost a fortune."

"You and your fancy hotels, Mr. big shot. You just love to spend money. I'm not going on a boring vacation and spend a lot of money to be bored!"

She criticized the itinerary and decried the first class hotels as either not well situated or probably not worth the premium price. She expressed unhappiness with the entire trip and instructed me to cancel it or go alone. She was not going. I was devastated.

I called the travel agent to cancel. We had spent a lot of time planning the trip. Cissie did not want to be involved but she had read the literature and approved the itinerary after making revisions. The travel agent had done a great job and had accommodated the many changes before we finalized the itinerary. I had not told her Cissie was not well. She told me I would forfeit 50% of the price if I cancelled so close to departure.

I took this back to Cissie and convinced her she would have a good time. She finally agreed to go but insisted I change one more hotel.

Hanoi was a success. Cissie loved the hotel and the sightseeing. We went to local restaurants that were our want. The guide was excellent. We bought a piece of art and a beautiful housecoat for Cissie. I started to relax.

The trip went downhill from Hanoi. Cissie complained the weather was not great, some places were too crowded, and the food was not as good as on her earlier, less expensive trip. She claimed disinterest and waited outside at the War and Remembrance Museum built by the North Vietnamese in Saigon after their victory. I had to see it as an American. I saw it alone. It was quite moving. She did not go on the famous motor scooter evening tour in Ho Chi Min city. She said she was too tired and not interested. I went alone; it was fabulous.

Angkor Wat was a success. Cissie fell in love with a handbag in Siem Reap. It is still her favorite. Then we flew home.

I was depressed and frustrated. I had worked hard to show her a good time. She had raved about her first trip to Vietnam. Some of her criticisms were valid. Vietnam was modernizing rapidly and its old charm was evaporating to modern life and architecture. But her adventurous spirit was gone and she drew little pleasure from places and things that once would have pleased her. I suspected this had been our last major trip.

Looking back, I became angry, too. I knew two guys amongst the pictures of the killed Americans on the displays at The War and Remembrance Museum. And the swift boat in the courtyard looked so inadequate for a river fighting ship by today's standards. My college roommate had served thirteen months on one, commanding a flotilla of three. He was a Navy lieutenant. He and his men had little armor and only a fifty-caliper machine gun on the bow of what looked more like a long rowboat than a war ship. They took and returned fire everyday and never once actually saw the enemy in the dense jungle on both sides of the Mekong. Cissie knew him and I would have liked to share these displays with her.

The Vietnam War was a great American disaster and our generation had fought it. Even though I knew she was sick she could have accompanied me throughout the museum. She knew it was important to me. Her refusal reinforced my growing belief we could no longer share the interesting things in life together.

I did most of the worthwhile sightseeing essentially alone. I realized in Vietnam how alone I now was. Loneliness arrived in Vietnam.

Peter Barnet

Chapter 13

Florence

No sooner had we recovered from Vietnam travels and jet lag from the return than we were off again for a short trip to Italy. We were going to a wedding outside of Florence and decided to spend two days there beforehand

Several of us from the Pan Am group in Paris were going. (The bride's mother was an active member.) They were also going to Florence first but were staying a bit outside. I wanted our stay to be easy for Cissie. I booked a hotel in the heart of Florence, a ten minutes walk to La Ponte Vecchio. We could go everywhere by foot. The hotel was nice and not expensive.

We arrived around noon and walked around. It was a lovely April day and the city was breathtaking. We passed a nice-looking restaurant and made a reservation for dinner. I thought, *So far so good.*

We went back to our room around 5:00 pm for a nap before cocktails and dinner. We got into bed and slept for about forty-five minutes. Suddenly and out of the blue Cissie started to yell at me for picking a fancy hotel. The other Pan Am folks were outside the city in less expensive ones. I argued that we would all be together at the wedding. So I picked a nice hotel in the city center for the two of us and we didn't have to bother with taxis, etc. And Florence was so romantic. This was perfect.

Cissie was not assuaged and was verbally abusive for some minutes. Her look was cold on one hand and indifferent to my pleading on the other. I had tried to please her but her behavior and look was what might have been appropriate had she just learned that I was having an affair.

The storm passed and we went downstairs to the bar for cocktails. Cissie was now calm and pleasant. But I was shaken and again feelings of being alone returned, this time mixed with a little desperation. Her outburst was for nothing. Oh, this dreadful disease!

I remembered how much Cissie had enjoyed our tour of Lombardy a few years earlier. We had stayed at similar hotels and immersed ourselves in the wonders of Italian culture. I wondered if this was our last trip to Italy. It was.

We had a good time in Florence and then went out to the suburbs for the wedding. We stayed in a small hotel in the village with some friends from Pan Am. We drove with them to the church and later to the reception and dinner. On our way there we reflected on marriage and weddings with the other couple in the car. I asked them how long they had been married. They answered.

Cissie was in the back seat and broke in. "Peter," she said, "how long have we been married? It's twenty years, right?" She was looking for affirmation because she did not seem certain.

Our friends looked surprised.

I made a joke. "Yes, we are married twenty years and remember how happy we were that Chris could come to our wedding. He was sixteen." Everyone laughed except me inside. "Actually dear we will be married forty years in June." Cissie said, "Oh, that's right."

I think our friends thought this was just fun repartee between Cissie and me.

It wasn't.

Cissie in Florence with the Ponto Veccio in the background, 2016

Peter Barnet

Chapter 14

Visby and Second Visit

As 2016 progressed, Cissie and I summer vacationed in Sweden again. We went to the island of Gotland in the Baltic Sea. Our hosts were Swedish friends we knew from both Paris and Stockholm. Gotland is a wonderful summer island. It has a microclimate that gives it twice as many sun days as mainland Sweden. It has golf courses and beaches and many quaint old churches and a medieval town called Visby.

The ambiance of Visby is like stepping back one thousand years in time. Every summer in late July Visby has a two-week festival that recreates its medieval past. The town's people dress up with authentic copies of the clothes worn in the eleventh century. Vendors offer food from recipes of that time as well as amusement games that were then popular for both children and adults. At the end of the festival they put on a mock battle between rival armies on horseback. It is fabulous.

Our friends lived about twenty minutes by car from Visby near the sea on the side of the island facing north toward mainland Sweden. They are next to an active sheep farm. They have a friend who plays an antique 1952 accordion that he would play at evening parties. And when he did, the sheep in the grass next door would perk up and come over to the fence with big eyes to listen. Cissie and I were totally charmed.

Cissie's acid reflux plagued her during our stay. She was unable to participate in some outings and holed up in bed in their guest cottage. She was less vivacious than in earlier summer visits and spoke less at social evenings and dinner parties. She remained chatty with our friends at breakfast and daytime activities with them. She was beginning to lose weight. Her figure was naturally slim but she was becoming too thin. Never a big eater, she now ate even less. However, no one really noticed that something was wrong.

In September 2016, we returned to the neurologist for our second visit. He asked Cissie the same questions. Her responses did not go as well as the previous year. Her answer surprised him when he asked what season started in late September. She said Sweden did not have seasons other than midsummer (June 21).

Cissie had another MRI and cognition test in the following weeks. The MRI was unchanged but the cognition test indicated further deterioration. As a result, the doctor ordered a spinal tap.

Some neurologists recommend spinal taps because the fluid has enzymes that are more predictive of Alzheimer's than MRI scans of the hippocampus. Again, Cissie did not resist and exhibited only mild curiosity at the results. The doctor told me they were "borderline" but he thought we were looking at Alzheimer's in its early stage. Again, I asked him how much time. He thought three to four years.

Now our lives began to really change. Until now Cissie's developing problem had forced us merely to slow down. Few friends had picked up on it so our social life continued pretty much normally. However, our domestic life began to evolve.

I took over more and more of the daily food shopping and much of the cooking. We were kitchen people and cooked dinner together when home, chatting about the day's events and often catching the evening news on the kitchen TV. If historically Cissie stood in front of the stove cooking and I sat at the little kitchen table chopping or shredding or just sipping my wine, we now reversed positions. I cooked and Cissie sat sipping her wine. More and more she wandered off into the bedroom to lie down and I cooked alone.

More and more we ate in front of the TV in the den as opposed to the dining room. I think Cissie found it easier. I would ask her where she wanted to have dinner. She would say in front of the TV and always with the rationale that we had already talked in the kitchen. What more was there to talk about? Cissie never liked TV.

Chapter 15

Tougher and Tougher

Cissie went regularly to the Swedish Club both day and night. It was fifteen minutes from the apartment on the metro with one change of train line. This could not have been easier and the metro exit lay directly across the street from the club. She had done this for years. But by 2017 I began to take her there and pick her up. I asked some of her friends to make certain she came home in a taxi if I could not pick her up.

Cissie was embarrassed and furious with me for arranging it. She knew she had a problem but wanted to keep it private.

"You are ruining my reputation at the Club," she yelled. "My problem is my problem. It's none of their business."

My fiercely independent wife did not want to be seen as an invalid. I didn't blame her, but what could I do?

Cissie offered a solution. I should write out the directions to the club back and forth to the apartment and then test-market the directions with her on the metro.

We did this regularly after that and it sort of worked but by now she could not always remember our trial runs.

At one point Cissie wanted an appointment with a famous hairdresser in Paris. His salon was on the other side of the city and required two changes on the metro. I had a conflict the day and time of the appointment. Three days before we had spent several hours on the metro testing my written directions and her ability to do this. It went OK but I suggested she take a taxi both ways. That would take the anxiety out of the trip...for us both.

She refused. Cissie viewed taxis as a waste of money and even though this hairdresser cost a fortune and was worth it to her, the taxi was not.

But she was very nervous about taking the metro alone. The night before her appointment, she woke me at 3:00 am. She could not sleep over worries about getting lost on the metro. "I can't do it!" she cried.

Again, I begged her to take a taxi. I begged her to let me reschedule it. She refused. She no longer wanted to go. The challenge had overwhelmed her so I canceled the appointment. It was so sad.

Our apartment building installed a new security system with an interphone and camera. We would buzz people in and could see them when they rang up from both the outside and an inside door. Our unit to do this was installed next to the front door to the apartment. It was standard stuff and easy to use. It was also a great security improvement.

Cissie simply could not master it despite written instructions and a big red sticker I placed next to the buzzer button. Further she was beginning to have difficulty turning the TV on and off.

Our lives were changing, indeed.

Our active involvement in the Pan Am World Wings Club also began to change.

I suspect this club is unique and in many ways extraordinary. Pan Am is long gone but in its heyday it was an iconic airline, a pioneer of modern commercial aviation. The flight attendants kept this cache and their pride going by forming the club. We went to parties at least once a month, participated in travel excursions to other European cities, special weekends in fun places in France, and more. Cissie and I loved the whole thing. We had as many as fifty people for cocktail dinatoires at our apartment. Everyone brought something. It was great.

By 2017, these big gatherings at home were no longer possible. What had been great fun for Cissie was now great stress for Cissie. We saw less and less of the Pan Am crowd.

Cissie was not the only Swedish girl to seek adventure in the world. But as far and wide as Swedish ladies built their diaspora, they guarded their Swedish identities and culture.

They formed a ladies educational club that assured this. SVEA had chapters worldwide and annual gatherings both locally and internationally. Cissie would go on a trip once a year with SVEA

Europe. One year, the ladies went to Tunisia for ten days. Picture about fifty blonds riding fifty camels in the desert. Ladies and beasts looked color coordinated. You can't make this stuff up.

Cissie toured Europe with SVEA and always roomed with a close friend whom she had originally met in Le Vesinet. They always came home smiling. Clearly, they had a wonderful time. To know Cissie was to understand how important her Swedish identity was to her and how she loved theses annual excursions with SVEA

Her final SVEA trip was to Portugal in 2017. She went with her usual friend but she had to return to Paris alone. We spoke daily and it became increasingly clear that Cissie was worried about travelling alone.

"Peter, what if I get lost? Can you fly down to pick me up? Oh why did I come?"

This once intrepid globetrotter now feared finding her way through two airports and with taxis on either end. Another SVEA member saw her distress and volunteered to take her to the airport. She was flying to Paris, too. Cissie was enormously relieved but I knew her growing anxiety about getting home safely had ruined this beloved SVEA trip for her. It would be her last.

2017 dawned with a February winter holiday to Palm Beach, Florida. I booked the trip because our oldest American friends retired there and I believed Cissie would benefit from a warm climate. Further, I was determined to keep life going for her as much as possible and that was good for us both. She loved our friends and we were like family to each other.

We were planning to spend a week at their house and then visit another couple that we knew from Paris that lived near by.

Paris–Palm Beach is a long trip. We flew via Atlanta to West Palm Beach. It was becoming difficult to navigate Cissie through airports. They are difficult for everyone these days. But I could not leave her alone for a minute or she might wander off and she complained about everything. It was a bit like taking a child and stressful.

We arrived at our friends' house in late afternoon. It was not our first visit and they ushered us to the same downstairs guest room. We had a little siesta and came into the kitchen around 6:00 pm. About an hour later, Cissie excused herself to powder her nose.

Both our friends spun around and said to me, "So what's going on with Cissie?"

I played dumb to flesh out their question. They had other very close friends and had lived through the decline and death of the women from Alzheimer's. So their antennae were sensitized. They noticed Cissie seemed not to know their house and was not sure how to get to the guest bedroom.

So, I had to tell them. They handled it well. We talked a lot and they told me about their experiences with their now-deceased friend. One time they had lost her in London and were frantic. It ended OK but they never wanted to go through that again. Neither did I.

I woke up on our third morning with a dull pain in my right side. It got worse as the morning progressed. Our host took me to a local doctor who had a small emergency clinic with ultra sound and other diagnostic equipment. I had a kidney stone and my kidney was badly swollen. That pretty much derailed the next three days. Our hostess took good care of Cissie and with great sensitivity.

My friend told the doctor about Cissie. He gave me a lot of advice, some of which was helpful. He told me I was facing a disaster. That was not helpful; I already knew this.

We moved on to our friends from Paris. Cissie had formed a great friendship with the woman. They walked together for exercise several mornings a week on an island in the Seine and we saw a lot of them socially. I think the women was worried about Cissie but had said nothing.

Her husband and I took a ride on his boat one morning before meeting the girls for lunch. We got taking about age and it was clear he was probing. So, I told him and later that day I told his wife. They were both very upset but not surprised. And they could not have been kinder.

We returned to Paris in late February. The kidney stone had been a real bummer and the conversation about Cissie was sad. But the weather had been good and I think Cissie had enjoyed some of it. We resumed our Parisian lives but Cissie rarely went out alone now. She still knew Passy's shopping street but her girl friends took her to art club and conversation group meetings. And she was always relieved when they offered to do so. Otherwise she would not go. She was afraid she would get lost.

In March, I changed neurologists. I had lost confidence in the first one and upon references selected the head of the Neurology Department at The American Hospital. Cissie and I met him that month. I saw him alone first and again Cissie did not fuss. He had read her case records and was convinced she had Alzheimer's. He was 85% certain. But he wanted to have Cissie undergo a PET scan. He did not believe MRI's and spinal taps were sufficiently predictive. A PET scan was the best diagnostic tool.

He called me at home in the evening one week after Cissie had the test. She was in earshot and this time wanted to know the results. I mostly listened.

The doctor said he had been 85% certain prior to the PET scan; now he was 95% certain. Could I come to see him alone the following evening at 7:00 pm?

I said, "Of course."

Cissie asked if he had given me the results. I replied that they were not yet available, which is why he called. He knew we would be anxious. She accepted this flimsy excuse.

The next evening he told me that Alzheimer's was now his official diagnosis. She probably had three to four years before she would need institutionalization. During this period she would probably start losing her foreign languages. She would retain Swedish because native tongue memory is located in a different part of the brain.

We discussed whether it would make sense if we relocated to Stockholm because of language. He thought it would and suggested Cissie would be more comfortable in her native culture. He encouraged me to consider this seriously.

I asked him if he would tell Cissie she had Alzheimer's. I was worried about that because the word is terrifying. He agreed and told me I should not tell her. This was his job but he never used the term unless patients asked directly. He referred to their problem as "memory disease" if they did not.

I began to consider moving to Stockholm.

Coincidently, the 2017 edition of Figaro's, "Best Bed and Breakfast Hotels in France," arrived in newsstands the same week. Its cover featured a fabulous looking place near Uzes in le Gard. The B&B was new and had been the summer home of Jean-Louis Trintignent, the male lead in *A Man and a Woman* and a major French movie star of the '60s. We had made no summer plans but quickly agreed to book a week at this B&B in June. We knew the area and loved it.

A few days later Cissie received an invitation to Le Cote d'Azur.

Her closest Swedish friend in France, the one she had met in Le Vesinet twenty-five years before and her SVEA travels roommate, had a home overlooking the Mediterranean in Bandol. This is a small, picturesque seaside village arranged around a sailboat harbor about forty-five minutes east of Marseilles. Her friend's house is high up at one end of the village over looking the island headquarters of spirits distiller, Pernod Ricard.

Her friend asked her to come for a week in late May because her husband was going on a weeklong regatta with a crew of eight. She thought the two girls could have a good time together and get caught up on things. And she knew Cissie loved the Cote d'Azur. She also knew that something bad was going on with her friend but I had not yet discussed it with her.

Cissie was genuinely excited and I was determined that she should go. The question was: how? One way was for me to take her there by plane or train and then return to Paris, or, alternatively, stay on my own for a week and then pick her up.

Her girl friend and I analyzed our options. Finally we agreed that I would put Cissie on the TGV high-speed train to Marseilles. There she would have to make a change to a local one to Bandol, but this was not complicated. We worked out all the details; I wrote them down for Cissie. She was still able to work her cell phone. I would call her regularly during her train ride and change at Marseilles. Her girl friend would do the same. Then I would come down to pick her up and drive to Jean-Louis Trintignant's former house if I could change the reservation at the B&B.

This worked out. Further, I decided that after Uzes we should drive the Cote d'Azur to Nice and rent an apartment there for two weeks. We would stop for two nights at La Croix Valmer, a fabulous seaside town we had visited before. This would assure no driving day with more than two–three hours in the car. Cissie loved Nice and wanted a place there. This was now impossible but at least she could have one last holiday there.

I took Cissie to le Gare Lyon to put her on the train. She had a first class ticket for a single seat next to the window. The conductor made an exception to let me settle her into her seat and organize the logistics of ticket, phone, written instructions, luggage, magazines, bottled water, and snacks. She was calm and again I felt like I was putting a child on the train. We kissed and I left.

I parked myself at the entrance to the platform and waited for the train to pull out. I watched it leave the station with my poor damaged Cissie on it. This would be her last voyage alone. I turned to head for the metro and then I lost it. I turned back to look at the empty platform and train track. I started to cry.

Happily, Cissie made the trip and the change at Marseilles without incident. I was enormously relieved. She had a wonderful week with her girl friend. They took long walks by the sea every day and went out twice for dinner in local restaurants. Her friend cooked the other evenings. It was a quiet week but a time of happiness for Cissie because she felt safe and unthreatened. I was increasingly seeking ways to make her happy, knowing the clock was ticking.

I picked her up at the end of the week and we drove to the B&B. A very attractive couple from Normandy had taken it on and the woman was a fabulous cook. The whole place was charming. We had a good week, which passed without incident.

We headed down the Cote d'Azur to La Croix Valmer. The trip was stressful because I made a wrong turn and we were lost for a while. Cissie did not handle that well and neither did I. When we finally reached our hotel, Cissie was starting to get her acid reflux, the hotel was unattractive, and a mistral was blowing. This is heavy wind that comes down the Rhône river valley and is very unpleasant.

We had dinner the first night in the hotel restaurant at the beach behind protective glass, but the mistral made everything shake and caused a lot of noise.

Cissie spent the next day in bed and I had to cancel a dinner invitation from a French couple we knew in Paris who had a summerhouse in the area. I had dinner alone.

We drove onto Nice and moved into the rented apartment two blocks inland from Nice's famous waterfront Promenade des Anglais. Cissie stayed in bed another two days until her acid reflux subsided.

For the next ten days, we walked down the Promenade every morning until we reached old Nice. This is the tourist area with charming old buildings and streets, restaurants everywhere, and way too many tourists in summertime. We had lunch there everyday, visited Nice's famous open air market, and walked back up the Promenade in the afternoon. We spent most evenings at home with a light supper and went early to bed. Our world was shrinking more and more. We did go to the Chagall Museum. It was fabulous and the highlight of the trip.

Our summer adventures had gone pretty well all things considered but I knew we would never do that again.

Cissie in the garden at La Croix Valmer
on La Cote d'Azur, 2007

As we approached autumn, I was increasingly nervous about more upcoming travel. We had accepted a wedding invitation in Charlottesville, Virginia from close friends we knew originally from Paris. Their younger daughter was getting married and they had put together a full weekend for about two hundred guests. They had no idea Cissie was sick.

We had to go to New York first for administrative reasons. I had booked a room at The Yale Club across the street from Grand Central Station. We planned four nights and arranged dates with family and old friends. Cissie was well rested before we left. After New York, we had scheduled a short flight to Charlottesville and a return flight out of Washington to Paris.

After two nights at The Yale Club, Cissie announced she was not going to the wedding in Charlottesville. It was too much trouble and would be boring. I could go alone or cancel it but she was not going. She became abusive. "All you care about is going to fancy parties and playing the big man. And you don't care if you drag me around when I'm not feeling well as long as you can be the life of the party...and I hate it here. I hate The Yale Club!"

I knew this was probably too much for Cissie and that her criticizing the wedding was driven by her worries about her ability to handle it. But we had to come to New York anyway and I really wanted to go to this wedding. I pushed back hard and insisted we go. "These are very good friends of ours and they will be furious if we don't come at the last minute. This is supposed to be a happy thing. Don't spoil it for me and I promise you'll have a great time!"

Eventually, I prevailed, and we flew to Charlottesville. Cissie got into the spirit and indeed had a good time. The wedding was splendid and we were seated with lovely people at the dinner. Cissie engaged in conversation with the man sitting next to her and it looked as if they were both having a good time. I was pleased and relieved.

The final event was Sunday brunch at a hotel before we took a taxi to Dulles Airport. It was a stand-up affair with an open bar and buffet. Cissie and I were standing near the bar sipping our wine when her dinner partner approached to say how much he had enjoyed their dinner conversation. Cissie was pleased. He began talking to me and in midconversation she interrupted with a completely unrelated and out of the blue thought. It was bizarre.

The man was startled and said, "What?"

I laughed and made a lighthearted remark to get past this moment.

Later in Paris, I emailed our hostess, raved about the wedding, and then told her about Cissie. She did not reply immediately but her husband wrote me later that day. They were devastated and offered all their love and support to us both. Two days later she wrote to say she was speechless and terribly upset.

Peter Barnet

Chapter 16

Getting Help & Going Public

Well before our trip to Charlottesville, I had crossed the bridge to getting help for myself. Cissie was becoming a full-time job and I was her primary caregiver.

In December 2016, I emailed a classmate from boarding school days who had lived a similar expatriate business life and was now living in Chicago on the verge of retiring in Montana. He had written me the year before to tell me his wife had Alzheimer's and he had been forced to put her in a home in Bozeman. "I've been her primary caregiver for three years now and I can't do it anymore," he wrote. I did not really understand why; boy would I learn.

He knew Cissie as he and his wife had lived in Paris several years earlier and we had seen them socially. We were now both in the same boat but he was further down the road.

He wrote me right back and we agreed to talk by phone. We had to navigate an eight-hour time difference. I would call him from a café in Passy so Cissie would not know. We began an email and periodic phone relationship (calls lasting ninety minutes). He is a true friend and has been there for me ever since. We had a bond from boarding school but Alzheimer's cemented it. We are brothers in the same nightmare. I will always be in his debt.

In our first call he advised me to get a psychologist.

Later he told me the story of the day he put his wife in care: "We flew from Chicago to Bozeman. Out home is eighty miles away from the city. She thought we were going on a vacation and on the plane she expressed that it would be nice to see the house again. When we arrived at the airport, I told her I had to pick something up in Bozeman before going home. The memory care folks were waiting for us and told me it would be best if I left immediately after we arrived at the home and tell my wife I would see her soon. I should not come back for a week. I did as instructed. My wife had no idea where she was, who these people were, or why she was there. She had a fit when she realized I was leaving her. I started to drive home but after a mile, I pulled over to the side of the road and cried like a baby for half an hour. I was in utter despair and racked with guilt."

I have never forgotten one word of what my classmate told me.

Both my doctor and our neurologist echoed my friend's advice about getting a psychologist.

My first reaction had been protest. "I don't need a psychologist; there's nothing wrong with me."

"Trust us Peter, no one can manage this challenge alone. You have to have someone to talk to who can help you blow off steam. Otherwise you will blow up."

In early 2017, I started to see a psychologist once a week. He specialized in treating primary caregivers and well understood the psychological dynamics of Alzheimer's for them. He talked a lot about stress management, and finding private time for myself. He emphasized that I should have a walk alone every day for at least forty-five minutes if private time was not possible on any given day.

During an early session, I expressed my sense that a happy old age was no longer possible for me.

He said something that stuck: "Peter, at this point in your life and given your wife's affliction, you should not be looking for happiness; you should be looking for meaning."

This impressed me. He was telling me that this was the time to reflect on our lives and our values, to assess the worthiness of our lives and how we felt about how we had lived. There was still time to go out with friends for a steak dinner but it was more important to determine whether I felt good about my life and why. Meaning would in fact create happiness.

We agreed I needed help at home, someone who could occupy Cissie at least once a week to allow me some real time off. There were many such services in Paris. However, they were French and Cissie was losing all interest in speaking French. Ideally I needed a Swedish solution.

I made an appointment with the deacon at the Swedish Church. It plays a major role in Swedish expatriot life in Paris. The deacon had organized a group of older ladies to assist aging Swedes who needed help at home. I profiled Cissie for him so that he could select the right person for her. This could only work if the ladies liked each other and shared common interests such as business and finance or art.

We met again a few weeks later with the woman he thought would be a good fit. She had met Cissie but they were not friends. However, they did have mutual friends. I was delighted. At this time Cissie was still trying to hide her problem from her Swedish pals and would have rejected any organized companion effort.

We settled on a ploy to pull this off. One of Cissie's closest girl friends would invite Cissie, and some other ladies including the volunteer to a luncheon at her apartment. The two would meet in a social atmosphere and hopefully hit it off.

Cissie's girlfriend lived near by.

It worked like a charm. The ladies met, the luncheon was a success and the woman from the church walked Cissie home. Cissie bubbled to me about this lovely and interesting lady she had met at her girlfriend's luncheon. She thought it was such good luck to make a new Swedish friend at her age. She never knew that we had arranged it at the church and never would. Now she had a companion. They had a coffee or lunch once a week at our apartment and then went walking together. It worked well. Most of Cissie's girlfriends still did not know about her illness. They knew something was wrong but thought it could just be age. Her new companion knew, of course.

A single lady friend invited us to dinner before our trip to the states. We were five. The other couple were Americans whom we had not seen for sometime but had known for years. The woman was an accomplished medical psychologist. Cissie and I liked them a lot. Our hostess knew about Cissie and was a member of her conversation group.

We had a fine evening but Cissie did not talk much. The couple left first and the hostess and I agreed that they probably hadn't noticed anything. The next morning she called me to report that our psychologist friend had phoned to thank her and asked what was wrong with Cissie. Evidently, she had said to her husband as they left the dinner that she thought there was something wrong.

Cissie was different. Her eyes were different. She couldn't put her finger on it but Cissie had changed.

I called her and we had a long conversation.

"What made you think Cissie was different?" I asked.

"I first noticed during cocktails," she replied.

"You were talking to my husband and I was talking to Cissie. She told me she wanted to move to Stockholm. That was her dream. She kept repeating that every time she spoke despite our conversation having moved on. Early Alzheimer's victims express sentiments about home so I wondered a bit.

"Then during dinner, Cissie was sitting next to you and seemed uncertain about talking with us. She seemed to be looking to you for guidance or comfort or something. It was subtle but after our cocktail conversation I was watching her at dinner. She just wasn't the Cissie we know. My husband didn't pick this up but I've seen a lot of it in my professional life."

I confirmed it was Alzheimer's. That was the morning I knew I had to go public.

From the start I had felt and learned from others that when symptoms begin to show and our behavior socially starts to change (such as turning down invitations or no longer going to evenings at clubs or leaving dinners early) it was best to go public. Otherwise friends would speculate or think we didn't like them anymore. They could even become angry with us. But if they knew, they would rally and support us. This proved to be right.

As 2018, dawned our Swedish friends from Stockholm and Gotland who had been with us the night of the apartment fire asked us if we would like to join them for a cruise to Greece in the coming September. They knew we were thinking about moving to Sweden and wanted to launch us socially with friends who were joining them for the cruise.

We agreed to go but in the midst of the planning Cissie changed her mind again and refused. She explained the cruise was on too big a boat. She would only go if it were a small boat. The smaller cruise ships are far more expensive than the big ones. So this idea was not well received by our friends.

I felt like a jerk suggesting an outrageously expensive trip and asking eight people most of whom we barely knew or had not even met to rethink their holiday. Again, I was angry and frustrated and embarrassed and ashamed and terribly sad. I knew this was not Cissie; this was her disease talking. She was afraid of getting lost on a big ship. This terrified her. But that didn't change my fear that we had blown it with our wonderful friends who wanted to launch us socially in Stockholm. We cancelled.

The next morning I called them at their apartment in Paris. He had left for Stockholm but she was there. I asked if I could come over, as I wanted to tell her something. She agreed but I could tell she was apprehensive. I told her that Cissie had Alzheimer's and was terrified to find her way around a big cruise ship. She let out a cry when I told her.

Most of our friends knew by now and I informed the remaining ones in the coming weeks.

Peter Barnet

Chapter 17

Stockholm

I now had a plan. We would take 2018 to decide whether we should move to Stockholm. This was an enormous decision with many moving parts. First we had to determine the feasibility of living in Sweden. If that looked OK we would test-market living there over the summer, investigate where to live, look at apartments, and decide whether buy or rent. If that went well, we would make a decision in the fall, put our Paris apartment on the market, and target a spring 2019 relocation.

Certainly, I was apprehensive. Moving to a new country and language with a sick wife at our age could only compromise my own. Most of my closest friends who knew about this thought I was nuts—noble but nuts. I thought it was best for Cissie and would give her a little happiness and comfort before Alzheimer's overwhelmed her. She would have to go into a memory care home eventually and a Swedish one would be better than a French or American one for her.

Some friends and family advised I put her in a home in Stockholm and move myself to Florida. I could go to Stockholm once a quarter to visit her. That would mean essentially abandoning my wife...like a rat abandoning a sinking ship. Cissie's ship was sinking but I was not a rat. This idea was impossible for me.

I took the winter and spring of 2018 to determine the healthcare, financial, and legal implications of making this move. There were tax issues, family law issues, and some immigration issues for me. Cissie's long-term care was paramount, particularly because she would eventually go into a memory care home. I had to do this thoroughly and would need professional advice and counsel.

I hired Price Waterhouse to analyze the tax ramifications of moving to Sweden and identified a lawyer in Stockholm to advise me on Swedish residency requirements, access to the healthcare system, wills, inheritance, and more. I was an American; Cissie was a Swede; and our son, who now lived and worked in London, had dual citizenship with the US and Sweden. This whole project had a lot of moving parts, indeed.

Cissie had no idea I was doing all this and would not have had interest in the details at this stage. She wanted to live in Stockholm.

I was incredibly fortunate to have a Swedish friend in Stockholm to make all these contacts possible. He identified PWC's office there and the family lawyer.

He knew a lot about the healthcare system, and real estate. He had just retired as chief executive of a successful company and was now active on many boards including hospitals and nursing homes. He and his wife had no idea about Cissie's illness. He was a godsend for me.

I put all this in motion. It was phase one of the plan.

We started the year with another trip to Palm Beach, Florida

We had to go to the states to sign new wills and I wanted Cissie to have some warm weather to break up the winter.

I planned it as a repeat of our 2017 two-week stay with the same two couples. However, with two exceptions: no kidney stones and no changing planes in Atlanta. We would fly Paris–Miami round trip and drive back and forth to Palm Beach. I booked one night at a Miami airport hotel when we arrived from Paris.

After the drama of Cissie's business class confusion discussed earlier, we arrived in Miami after a very pleasant flight in comfortable seats and with wonderful service. By the time we rented the car and found the airport hotel, we were exhausted. We went straight to bed.

We were set to drive up to Palm Beach, a ninety-minute drive, in the morning, but during the night, Cissie suffered a return bout of her acid reflux. The combination of jet lag and the reflux made it impossible for us to go. She spent the day in bed miserably and I secured another night in our hotel room.

Sunday morning her reflux was better but she had developed a mild fever. The flu was particularly vicious this year. There was no way we could visit our friends and bring them the flu. Cissie needed a doctor but driving to the nearest clinic was tricky without GPS.

The hotel had a doctor contact who would come over. He charged $1,200 for a Sunday call and arrived at noon dragging two enormous suitcases. They contained a pharmacy, testing kits, and stethoscope, etc. I had never seen anything like it. I thought, *what a racket!* But he proved to be competent. Cissie did not have the flu. She just had jet lag. Her fever was gone. He gave her some Tylenol and vitamins and gave me a sympathy discount on his fee. We drove to Palm Beach.

Cissie stayed in bed another day and I played some golf with my host and two other guys. I could not hit a ball and pretty much inconvenienced the others. It was awful. On the 17th hole, one of the guys asked me what I had done for a living before I retired.

I answered, "I was a golf pro."

They all laughed and my buddy cracked up. Humor is always a good idea in tight spots.

Cissie was up and about the next day and we went to sign and notarize our American wills. Then at the end of the week we moved over to the other couple's place. They had planned a dinner at home. It went fine but our host was sniffling.

The following morning, our girl friend greeted us in the kitchen with the news that her husband and come down with the flu. He had a high fever and all the lovely symptoms that come with it. I called Air France and booked us back to Paris that evening. We could not stay in a flu house and further burden our friends. And Cissie wanted to go home. I didn't blame her. We returned to Paris after five days in Palm Beach. The whole trip was a nightmare.

Cissie and I were happy to be home and we quickly resumed our shrinking world routines. I did the shopping, the laundry, and the cooking. Cissie rose at 9:30 each morning, napped from 4:00–6:00pm, and retired at 9:30 if we were not watching a film that kept her attention. Her memory was so poor that I had to repeat everything multiple times daily.

"What time are we having dinner?"

"7:00 pm."

"What time are we having dinner?"

"7:00 pm."

"What time are we having dinner?"

"7:00 pm."

I was a member of the Board of Trustees of the American School of Paris. We scheduled board meetings monthly in the evening. I partnered with another trustee on the Advancement Committee. She was a widow and past president of the board. Once at an annual school wide function including spouses, I got separated from Cissie and stood next to my board partner during a speech.

Cissie stood alone. She resented my talking to this lady on the phone at home on board business and after the separation at the function saw her as a rival. She made a terrible fuss when we went home and forbade me to speak to the woman on the phone in the apartment. I had to go out and call her from the street. I tried in vain to convince Cissie that my board partner was not more important. Paranoia is a symptom of advancing Alzheimer's.

It was becoming difficult to go to board meetings because Cissie would forget where I was and badger me to come home. This would exacerbate if the meetings ran late as they frequently did. After one meeting that ended late I came home to discover that Cissie had locked me out. I had left her in the afternoon and had told her I would be late. She was in good spirits that day. We had gone out for lunch and I had prepared a smoked salmon dinner for her. She seemed OK with me going to the meeting. However, she had forgotten all this and was furious when I was not home by 9:30 pm.

I rang the bell and phoned her but she refused to answer. I did not want to create a scene in the hallway so I spent the night in a hotel and came back at 7:30 am. She had unlocked the door. I gave her hell and told her if she did that again I would call the police and she could pay to have the door repaired. She never apologized.

The following month I had to make a proposal to my fellow board members and ASP administrators on an important change to our communications program. Cissie called me just as I was beginning and made a terrible fuss. I had to take the call to make certain she was not going to run out of the apartment. She would not let me end the call. I excused myself to the board, stepped outside to calm Cissie down and returned to the meeting, embarrassed. The presentation went fine and my colleagues were gracious but inside I was all turmoil, *frantic*.

I called my partner from the street the next morning and told her Cissie had Alzheimer's.

She said, "I was afraid of that and praying I was wrong."

She agreed not to tell the other members. I did not want to compromise my effectiveness on the board. I considered and rejected resigning from it. I had already given up teaching. My activities were shrinking and that was not healthy. The neurologist was emphatic that I should pursue as normal a life as possible. That meant less time care giving and more time outside the apartment away from Cissie. I would stay on the board and maintain my partnership with my lady colleague who had become a treasured friend.

Stickers here, Stickers there, Stickers everywhere

Cissie possessed fine administrative skills. She kept excellent files on all subjects. She kept to-do lists and shopping lists. She was organized. Her closet was organized; her jewelry was organized. Her desk was organized. Alzheimer's now relentlessly took these virtues away from her. She compensated for her cognitive decline by buying a lifetime supply of Post It pads and putting stickers everywhere to help her cope with the mechanics of domestic life. She decided to do this when she realized she could not remember how to work the front door security system without a sticker to highlight which of the three buttons was the buzzer.

Never comfortable with the digital age, she now had trouble with our two televisions. She could not remember the two remotes that went with each.

They were identical. The TV remote turned on and off by pressing the red button, the cable box by pressing the green button. Both were located in the upper right hand corner of the remotes. So I wrote out the instructions and taped them to the kitchen and den walls by the TVs along with a list of the five channels we watched for news in English.

Cissie stickered the backs of the remotes, as well. She stickered all the kitchen appliances. She stickered lists everywhere as well as regularly used telephone numbers such as Chris's in London. She put favorite recipes on the walls and all scheduled appointments. This was easier for her than keeping her agenda book.

By 2018, Cissie could no longer manage her bank accounts with certainty. She had one in Passy and one in Stockholm. They were checking and investment accounts at both banks. Her companion from the Swedish Church was a retired chief financial officer and helped her with both accounts. She begged Cissie to give me permission to access and manage her accounts with her. She refused. Her independent character and growing paranoia fought this common sense initiative.

Cissie had a lovely banker at her local branch in Passy. She no longer wanted to go to the bank alone. He recommended she put me on her accounts as well. Again she refused. I listened to their dialogue about her investments and savings account and marveled at his patience, as it was obvious she was not well.

I told him afterwards and he allowed he'd thought Alzheimer's was the case. He assured me he would make no transactions at her direction without alerting me first. Legally he could not stop her unless I had joint powers with the accounts. He begged me to convince her to give me access.

By spring, PWC pretty much assured me that moving to Sweden was a wash financially as remaining in Paris. I had made progress on family law issues but still needed to understand more about the Swedish healthcare system. However, I had enough to prepare for the summer in Stockholm.

I rented our friends apartment for six weeks beginning mid-July. It was in the most desirable neighborhood of Ostermalm. And they invited us to come to Gotland for a week during our stay. They also let us use their apartment for a week in late May to set up some advance contacts with realtors and I wanted to see my helpful friend on healthcare details. Cissie was delighted to go to Stockholm in May.

We had a good week as planned. The May weather was delightful and we had a few nice evenings with our friends from Paris and others from our summers there. My CEO friend and his wife came back from a vacation toward the end of the week. I invited them to dinner at a lovely restaurant and we were able to sit outside on a particularly glorious evening. Stockholm is so far north that there is little night in May and if the weather is good it is very special.

We met at the restaurant with big hellos and it was clear they were happy to see us and talk about our moving plans. We ordered champagne to celebrate our reunion and the beautiful evening. They told us about their vacation that had been so interesting. Cissie sat next to the lady with a good view and we guys sat opposite looking toward the wall of the restaurant.

Dinner was great. The girls talked a bit to each other and we guys did the same. We ordered desert and Cissie excused herself to go to the ladies room. She seemed uncertain as to how to find it and the lady gave her directions.

When Cissie was gone, she asked how I was.

I said, "Great!"

"And how is Cissie?" she said seriously.

I asked why her question was so serious, had she noticed something? Swedes are direct. She said Cissie sounded like her mother who had Alzheimer's and had died a few years ago. The mood at the table changed dramatically.

I told them where we were with Cissie's illness and then she came back to the table. They handled it very well. My friend and I talked in the morning and agreed to next steps and meeting again in July. They were very sad and when I told our other good pals in Stockholm they were all devastated.

I took Cissie for a check-up with the neurologist before we returned to Sweden for the summer. He estimated she was two–three years away from a memory care home.

We arrived in Stockholm for the summer in early July. This is the vacation month in Sweden and Stockholm is empty. Many restaurants are closed. I intended to use the first two weeks to visit friends in other places and take Cissie on boat rides throughout the Archipelago. It is summer heaven with 24,000 islands from a rock to big islands.

We moved into the apartment at Karla Plan. This is ground zero for desirable locations about a twenty-minute walk to the harbor and the center of postcard Stockholm. It is also a summer paradise with waterside restaurants on boats.

My plans to visit other areas and friends in other cities did not happen, as Cissie couldn't make the effort. We saw a few friends and visited some in the archipelago. Most days we followed a recurring regime.

Cissie rose around 9:30 am as usual and was ready to go out around 11:00. We then walked into town to a square by the harbor and to an Asian fusion restaurant called East. It was very popular with a lovely outdoor terrace. Cissie ate very little at this point and had lost too much weight. But she loved a Japanese rice dish at East and ordered it every time. This is why we went there three–four times a week. I enjoyed it, too.

After lunch we would look in shop windows and then walk back to the apartment via the harbor. We would be home by 3:30 pm. Cissie would lie down for a nap and get up around 6:00. I would go to the store to buy food for dinner and cook. Or we would go to a tapas restaurant on Karla Plan. We were in bed by 9:00. It was a replay of Nice the year before.

I felt old...like an old man only fit to sit in the park and feed the birds, read the newspaper, and watch television after dinner. I was caught in Cissie's shrinking world. She had no choice but I did. But I despaired that I could not escape without leaving her, and as I have said, that was out of the question for me. She would have to go into a care home before any real return to a normal life was possible for me. The constant presence of Cissie's disease in our home life sapped much of my energy to pursue other normal interests.

In F. Scott Fitzgerald's novel *Tender is the Night*, the protagonists are an American couple on the French Riviera. The wife has just returned from a sanitarium. The doctor tells the husband, who will have to care for her at home, "beware of the tyranny of the weak." He warns that they can drag the strong one down by consuming their caregiving lives. I worried this was true. I mused about our wonderful summers in the archipelago. They were gone for us.

...

Fagelbro, Stockholm Archipelago, July 2008

"We're lucky with the weather this year; it's a perfect night for our party!"

"How many are we again?" I asked.

"Ten in the red cottage with the long table," Cissie replied.

We had been preparing all day. Cissie had gone down to the wharf to buy warm smoked salmon from the Saturday Lax Boat. It came twice a week, a water going fishmonger and fabulous. Cissie could walk there from our cottage. I took the car to the supermarket to buy the other stuff and then drove back, stopping at a roadside vegetable stand to buy strawberries. They are really special in July in Sweden.

It was going to be a grand evening, our annual summer party for our friends whom we so enjoyed seeing every year. They loved white wine and I had made certain we would not run out.

July is vacation month in Sweden. It never gets really dark and everyone is in a festive mood after the long dark winters in Scandinavia. Cissie was no exception.

She loved the archipelago, loved our friends, some whom she had known since her stewardess days in New York, and this was her big night to shine. She glowed.

The evening was filled with laughter and Cissie was tireless. At 1:00 am we grilled hot dogs, a Swedish summer party tradition. Since it never gets dark, the party never ends. We got to bed around 3:00 am.

Summers in the Stockholm Archipelago:
Peter & Cissie in July 2008 and Cissie in July 2010

Stockholm, July 2018,

We looked at real estate and saw a fabulous place, but it was premature. Nevertheless, we settled on Ostermalm as the place to live. We had a few varied days with museums, long walks, and an opera recital at the famous opera house overlooking the royal palace. And I insisted we take a boat trip in the archipelago. Mostly, it was walk into town, lunch at East, and walk home.

In early August, my CEO friend and I visited a memory care facility on the island of Sudemalm. He was on the board of this facility and his father was a resident there. It was perfect but had a long waiting list and we pretty much figured we would have to be Stockholm residents for two years before we could get a place for Cissie. The timing was OK, or so I thought.

My friend invited me for a sandwich lunch at his apartment. A girlfriend of Cissie's took her to lunch that day.

My friend came right to the point. He asked, "Peter, can you make this work?"

I wanted to listen to this able friend. "Tell me why you ask?"

"You have two to three years yet of living together. Life in Stockholm will be much reduced compared to Paris where you have built a full life."

I allowed I was worried about that.

He clarified, "I am not worried about you. You make friends easily. But Cissie's life will be lonely here. There's no Swedish Club and she will not be able to go out alone."

I translated, "What you mean is we will not have the social support and activities that we enjoy in Paris and we are damaged goods."

He said, "Yes."

I knew this was true but hearing this from him was sobering.

"My advice would be to maximize the time you have left together in Paris. These next few years are too precious to make them less than they can be for both of you."

Swedes are direct. It is a fine quality and he was a fine friend. I would think about it.

The following week we were to fly to Gotland. This local airport in Stockholm was fifteen minutes away. The flight itself only forty minutes and our friends were picking us up at the Visby airport. Cissie announced she did not want to go. She had no sympathy for the sunk cost of the tickets if we did not go or that we would hurt our good friends who had planned a party for us. She dug in her heels again and was abusive about everything and everyone.

I told our friends in Gotland and they both called to give Cissie confidence, assurances, and loving reasons to hold to course. This was to no avail. Over the next several days we were on and off several times and everyone was going crazy. At the last minute a realtor called to tell us he could not show us an apartment until the week after we had scheduled Gotland. Perhaps Cissie was looking for a way to save face. I don't know but she relented with the apartment visit delayed as an excuse and we flew to Gotland. Once there, she pulled it off pretty well.

We came home to Paris with me burdened as to the right or wrong of moving to Stockholm.

Chris came every six weeks on average to visit for the weekend when we were home. Cissie always looked forward to it deeply. But being a Swede she did not express this much. Sometimes, when Chris was in a playful mood, he would jump on her when she was resting and tickled her. She protested loudly every time, begging him to stop, but she was laughing at the same time, too.

One evening he pulled her out of bed in her bathrobe and started dancing with her in the library. He danced in an exuberant and devilish way and Cissie's smile outshone the sun. She was so happy to dance with her clowning son. She adored him, of course, and I was so pleased for her.

Peter Barnet

Chapter 18

September 20, 2018

It was a Thursday and a beautiful day in Paris. The fall has often-great weather in France's capital. I was looking forward to it because Cissie and I had a dinner date with American friends at one of our favorite restaurants in the 7th arr. I also had my first book group meeting of the 2018/2019 season at The American Library from 5:00–6:30 pm. The group leader and his wife were very much involved with ALP and we were having dinner with them afterwards at 7:00. The restaurant was around the corner from the library.

Cissie no longer went out alone except for short trips to stores in the neighborhood. It was too dangerous. I planned to get a taxi after the book group to pick her up and take us to the restaurant. This was now our new normal.

At 6:30, I said goodby to the group and told my friend we would meet at the restaurant as planned. I left the library, walked to the corner, and then to the left to a taxi stand nearby. I got into the taxi and gave the driver my home address and told him we would return to the restaurant with my wife. He said nothing and seemed a bit odd. I sat in my preferred spot in taxis, the backseat on the passenger side. I never put on the seat belt in the backseat.

The driver started up and proceeded to make a legal U-turn after the stoplight. It was actually a small circle letting onto several avenues. I was not concentrating but thought he was making the turn a bit fast. Suddenly, he lost control of the vehicle and drove us with speed into the center aisle traffic light. I had no time to react.

The traffic light post nearly cut the taxi engine in half. I was thrown forward violently and hit the front seat metal bar of the adjustable headrest with my mouth. My left hip hurt badly and I was dazed. The driver's face was covered in blood and I do not remember his airbag activating. My mouth was bleeding and I could not climb out of the car. Through the window and I saw people sitting close by in a crowded outdoor café. They looked at the crashed car and me with curiosity.

Many emergency ambulances in Paris are part of the city's fire department. It seemed one arrived immediately. A young fireman pulled me out of the backseat gently and laid me on a gurney. He took my ID and with his mate placed me in the ambulance. I was still dazed but able to call home.

"Hello, where are you?

"Cissie, I've been in a taxi accident near the library and I'm hurt. The ambulance is taking me to the emergency room at a hospital. I don't know which one."

"Oh my God! I'll come right away."

"No, stay where you are at home. I'll call you when I get to the hospital and know where I am."

"OK, but call soon and I'll wait by the phone. Are you going to be all right?"

"Yes, I'll be fine. but I think I'm hurt. I'll call as fast as I can."

Then I called the restaurant and got my friends on the phone. I asked them to take care of Cissie. They left immediately for our apartment and I prayed Cissie could buzz them in. Finally, I called Chris in London and we agreed he would catch the earliest Eurostar to Paris in the morning.

The firemen took me to the emergency room at a famous public hospital about fifteen minutes away with sirens blaring. Medical staff jumped on me. The doctor arrived and ordered morphine, an X-ray for my hip, and some one to sew up my lips. The blow had almost cut them in half and flattened my four bottom front teeth. They were still attached but lying on my tongue. The lips needed twenty-three stitches. Thank god for morphine.

After the X-ray they told me I had fractured my pelvis. It would be painful but it would heal on its own. They would see me again in the morning. I called Cissie to report on the diagnosis, and tell her that Chris would be at the apartment by 10:00 am. He would bring her to the hospital.

Our friends were great. He went out for a pizza dinner for three and she volunteered to spend the night. Cissie was frightened and worried and anxious but relatively calm. Our friend would not leave her until Chris arrived.

Cissie and Chris came to see me in the late morning. Poor Cissie didn't say much but wow was she stressed. Happily, Chris had taken charge of her and he took charge of me at the hospital. I really wanted to go home and the hospital agreed to discharge me after a dental visit. I had an afternoon appointment with the dentistry service to straighten my teeth and stabilize them, at least temporarily. They thought I would probably lose at least two. Chris skippered me through all the events and administrative stuff/discharge at the hospital. He had his arms around us both and he was furious with the taxi driver. He would not let this go by. He hired a lawyer and insisted I sue the taxi company. He worked with one of my friends to arrange everything for my return home.

At day's end, Cissie and Chris went home separately once the hospital put me in the ambulance. I could not stand up and it was very tricky hauling me up four flights. The elevator was too small. Thank god for morphine!

Chris and a friend found me a trained health care lady to tend to my needs. I could not get out of bed and Cissie was not the same girl who had wrapped the Sunday New York Times around my foot on our wedding night. The woman was willing to stay over night if needed but Cissie did not like that. After three days, I concluded I had to go to a rehabilitation clinic immediately. Home care was insufficient.

An ambulance hauled me to an orthopedic clinic in Boulogne. Going down the stairs was nightmarish. The clinic placed me in a private room. There was a doctor on each floor who kept all medical records and X-rays and a physical therapist came to my room daily. I was flat on my back and still on morphine.

Morphine is happy gas. It kills the pain and turns one into a comedian. I was one naturally so callers simply marveled that I was in such good spirits. Thank god for morphine. Cissie could not be alone at home and could visit me only if someone brought her. Several girlfriends agreed to take turns staying with her. She came once or twice to visit when Chris came from London on weekends. He came as much as possible and even worked from Paris one week.

Arranging help for Cissie was challenging. I spent at least an hour or more each day doing this and an hour at least on the phone with Cissie. She was in an increasingly terrible state. She would accept and then change her mind about friends staying with her. She would like them one day and hate them the next. She thought they were coming over to rob her or to drink our wine. She complained about being all alone and needed me home now. "They just want my money. They don't talk to me. They are throwing parties and don't invite me. I am all alone and don't know what to do. I am so unhappy. Can't you come home now? They just want my money. I am so unhappy. Oh, please do not hang up; please do not hang up."

Cissie would whine, complain, and plead in this manner daily and would not let me end the call. It was so pitiful. She never asked me once how I was. She was completely absorbed with her misery. Her entire performance was a litany of known behaviors of Alzheimer's patients as their disease progresses. It made things very difficult for me as I was flat on my back and on morphine. It was no fun for our friends who were rallying to help and stay overnight. I knew I was asking too much of them but I had no choice. Cissie would not have accepted a professional nurse or stranger in her home at this stage.

Further, I was not getting better and physical therapy was too painful. The therapist worried I would have a problem walking long-term unless I corrected the posture of my left foot. My right leg was normal so my right foot was vertical. But my left foot was lying flat on the bed staring into my right foot. Why this did not create greater concern with the doctor is beyond me. I was still on happy gas. It's dangerous stuff as we know and it was getting long.

One morning the physical therapist stopped when I screamed in pain and left the room. She came back with my X-ray and showed it to me. It looked as if my hip was not in its socket but I really could not tell and neither could she. The doctor looked at it as if for the first time and instantly ordered a MRI. I was hauled off again to a hospital for it. If you ever wondered what a sack of potatoes feels like I would be happy to tell you.

The doctor was waiting for me when we returned to the clinic. The hospital had called her. The MRI showed that my hip was broken and massively dislocated. She recommended surgery that evening at a partner hospital in Boulogne. However, I was really angry and called "time out." I wanted a specific surgeon at France's premiere orthopedic hospital near my home. They had helped me there before and I knew they were the best. Both the emergency room and the clinic had dropped the ball. Enough!

Three days later I had the surgery preformed at my chosen place. It was perfect. They returned me to the clinic two days after the surgery. I stayed there for a month, which is longer than usual because my leg muscles had atrophied after two weeks in bed. I had to rebuild them first and then learn how to walk again.

I returned from the surgery pain free and off the morphine. However, without it, the reality of a long rehabilitation and poor Cissie's malaise really hit me. I became depressed. I think I was beginning to feel sorry for myself. All the pain for two weeks before the surgery, the outrageous miss-diagnosis at the hospital emergency room, what seemed like a longer than normal recovery period learning to walk again, and Cissie's daily moaning and groaning all combined into a perfect storm of misfortune. And the future looked grim.

I was now on the clinic's geriatric floor and the doctor there took me in hand. "Monsieur Barnet, would you like to see a psychologist? I believe you could use some help." I declined and she continued, "You have a lot of baggage at this point and I understand you want to get home to take care of your wife. But if you don't stop talking to her so much and concentrate on your rehabilitation you will not get out of here quickly."

She was right, of course, but this was not easy. As the days passed, it became more and more evident that Cissie was descending deeper into an alternate reality. She complained that the Swedish girls who took turns staying with her were stealing her things, drinking our wine, and throwing wild parties to which she was not invited. She stopped eating and suffered from constipation. I begged her to eat more.

Her oldest friend from Copenhagen SAS days still lived there and volunteered to stay with Cissie for a week. This was another godsend. She flew to Paris and took good care of her, did all the shopping and cooking, took her for walks, and helped her with her stickers and telephone numbers. She cooked Swedish recipes for Cissie and even got her to eat a little bit. We talked daily but clearly she was more and more stressed each day. She was not well physically but nevertheless made this effort. I owed her a great debt.

Toward the end of my rehabilitation, I hired a younger Swedish woman to stay with Cissie and take her to doctors if necessary. She was not an ideal choice but I was out of bullets arranging coverage for Cissie. At times I thought I could start a new career at Bookings.com.

Cissie loved this girl one day and hated her the next. She started to panic over her constipation and insisted on going to our doctor, whose office was nearby. She did not want the girl to go with her and disregarded my pleas. She went out at 8:00 am to go on her own.

She called me a few minutes later in a panic. "Peter, you have to come right away! I don't know where I am. I forget how to get to the doctor and I don't know how to get home. You have to come get me right away. I'm so scared. You have to come!"

She had walked down our street and around the corner and was lost after having walked down that street every day for twenty-two years. More important she was terrified. And I could not come to her, of course. I was in the rehabilitation clinic.

I began talking to her in a soothing voice. "Calm down, sweetie. I'm here and will help you return to the apartment. Don't worry, nothing bad is going to happen to you. So let's get you home together with your iPhone. Are you ready? Yes? OK. Very good.

"Now tell me, where are you standing? Do you see the boulangerie? You do? Great! Now turn your back to the boulangerie and look across the street. Do you see the chocolate store on the corner? You do? Great! Now go to your left to the cross walk with the light. You are there? Now look at the light and wait until it turns green. It's green? Great! Now look to your right where the cars come from and cross the street. Are you now in front of the chocolate store? You are? Cissie you are doing great, really great! I am so proud of you. You are halfway home."

I coached her home by telephone flat on my back this way and the girl took her to the doctor later as planned. She was calm when she got home. I was exhausted and this was all happening before breakfast and physical therapy.

Later, Cissie believed she had saved me, arranging visitors at the clinic and coming almost every day herself to support me. Further, she thought she had been all alone during my absence. In reality, someone stayed with her every night and others took her out regularly during the day. She came to the clinic only three times.

I never disabused Cissie of this belief because doing so would have hurt her self-esteem. It was much better that she felt a hero. So, I thanked her profusely and regularly in the days and weeks ahead.

I returned home on October 31, another eventful Halloween in our recent lives. A friend drove me there in the early morning. He helped me upstairs with the luggage because I was still using a cane. I let us in and called to Cissie. She appeared at the far end of the foyer and my heart broke. She was so thin and so stressed and so scared, like a child who had been abandoned in a dangerous world.

The following week I took Cissie to the neurologist. I thought my accident and absence had sent her over a cliff. He allowed that my absence had pulled the rug out from under her. I was her world, but now that I was home, she would probably return to her previous state before the accident. He gave her some stronger medicines, including a mild sleeping aid. He was wrong.

I was shattered but glad to be home.

Peter Barnet

Chapter 19

Free Fall

It was great to be home...but it was not great to be the primary caregiver again. I had been through a lot in the past two months and Cissie had entered a challenging new phase.

I was pretty awful to her the first two weeks home. Everything she did and couldn't do annoyed me. I was in a foul humor and couldn't suppress my irritation and impatience. I criticized her constantly. "Don't tell me you lost your glasses again. I told you not to run the washing machine. We barely avoided a flood. Why are you dressed for dinner? It's only 3:00 pm. Look at this closet; it's a mess." And so on.

I was a long way from recovered. Doctors told me full restoration would take six–nine months. I put Stockholm on hold. Even if we went ahead, a spring move would be nuts. And would Cissie improve? Yikes!

I rehired the nice home caregiver to help with daily shopping as well as helping me sort through six weeks of mail, etc. She was multitalented and lovely but Cissie's paranoia identified a gold-digging woman out to steal me away. I was forced to let her go. This made my return much more difficult and I was angry at Cissie for making me do it.

Cissie pleaded with me to be nice to her when I became annoyed. Eventually I righted my unruly ship and returned to better humor. I was ashamed at my behavior to my very sick wife. I knew full well that Cissie couldn't cope anymore. It wasn't a fair fight anymore. I felt like I had abused her as one might treat a house pet badly. I felt like a bully and I detest bullies.

Cissie had rearranged her jewelry and her closet when I was away. This organized woman whose affairs were almost military in formation now appeared to have been victim of a ransacking. It took me two weeks to sort her jewelry and account for the real pieces among the large pile of mostly costume items. She fought to restore the "ransacked" approach.

Eventually, I secured the valuable jewelry in our safe and kept the keys. One good piece was missing and never found. One close friend who had stayed with her called to ask if I had seen her ring. She thought she had lost it in our apartment. I looked through everything and blessedly found it.

We had two keys to the basement storage cave. One was missing and Cissie accused the now fired home caregiver of trying to rob us. She must have the key.

"Call that women and tell her to bring it back or I'll call the police and have her arrested."

"Cissie, I swear to you she doesn't have the key. You are being unfair to her."

After much back and forth, I called the lady. She assured me she did not have it and had put it back in the front hall table drawer where we kept the keys. Cissie was relentless. She was unshakable in her belief that the girl was a thief and she had collaborated with her boyfriend to steal our valuables from the cave.

I had a copy made to appease her. Some time later, I found the spare in her blazer pocket whilst straightening her closet. Now we had three cellar keys.

We started looking for misplaced items two years before but this was different. Cissie was now hiding things to keep them safe. They weren't misplaced—they were hidden, but Cissie could not remember where. She could not remember she had hid them. She could not remember the item we were looking for. All the while I was taking physical thereby sessions at home. I no longer needed the cane.

We went back to the neurologist in mid-December. He was not happy with what he observed from Cissie and heard from my report of home life. He prescribed a tranquilizer and an antipsychotic. I gave Cissie only the tranquilizer. The antipsychotic scared me.

Christmas was approaching. The previous year, Cissie and I had celebrated in London with Chris and his future fiancée. We almost didn't go because Cissie tripped and fell on Le Champs Elyesee coming out of a movie the week before. It happened so fast I couldn't stop her. She fell right on her face.

By the next morning she looked like the loser in a boxing match—black and blue all over her face. Somehow we fixed her up. She agreed to go after promising her we would get a wheelchair and assistance boarding the Eurostar. She recovered quickly and I discovered that the fastest way to get from Paris to London was by wheelchair. We jumped the lines and had priority at security.

...

New York ,September 1980

Cissie was not certain she wanted a child. Her rheumatoid arthritis was raging and she was afraid of becoming an invalid. Having a child under that circumstance worried her. We discussed this with both her gynecologist and her rheumatologist. They felt that having a baby would give Cissie new purpose and lessen her chances of becoming invalided. Also, it was clear I wanted a child.

However, the process of conceiving would be a bit more complicated as they would have to wean Cissie off her arthritis medication. This would take about two months. The drugs Cissie was taking would probably prevent her from becoming pregnant and if she did conceive without being fully weaned from them would probably require an abortion, as the fetus would not be normal. However, once weaned and pregnant, the arthritis would disappear during her pregnancy, but sadly return after childbirth. Then she would have to go back on the medication. We decided to go ahead and try to have a baby.

Christopher was born on September 18, 1980. Cissie and I were 37. One month later, Cissie almost died from toxic shock. Her obstetrician had left some placental tissue inside her and it went off like a bomb. She spent a week in intensive care and made a full recovery but bringing our son into the world had been an above-average drama. Given her age and all this, we had no thought of having another. But we were thrilled to have Chris. Now we were a family of three.

...

Paris, December 2018

Chris and Tanya would come for five nights. We planned on going out for dinner with them on December 23rd: Christmas Eve at home with an aperitif first with close friends at home followed by Cissie's favorite Christmas smorgasbord for just the four of us after they left. Chris wanted turkey on Christmas day. He and Tanya would do the cooking. Boxing Day would be leftovers day and we had tickets to the Peking Circus's afternoon performance near le Parc Vincennes. This had been a tradition for us at Christmas time in Paris. We all loved it.

This was a well-paced schedule. We dispensed with another tradition: midnight mass on Christmas Eve at the Cathedral on Ile Saint Louis. Cissie had adored the church and the midnight service with a wonderful choir. Now, it was too much for her. It saddened me a lot. We faced a lot of cooking and too much food but this filled the holidays at home without putting any pressure on Cissie.

Our first night out in the restaurant went smoothly. Cissie enjoyed it but was a bit distant with Chris and Tanya. This continued throughout the day on the 24th but I was too busy to notice as I prepared the smorgasbord. Chris did not notice it either.

Last Christmas at Home with Chris and Tanya, 2018

At the aperitif with our good friends, I was surprised to see the husband shake his head back and forth and say to himself, "It is so sad."

We were sitting around the big coffee table in the living room; he was opposite from Cissie. I was serving the champagne. Our friends were regulars and intimate with Cissie's illness.

At the first chance, I asked him why he was shaking his head and was it about Cissie.

His response startled me. "Yes," he said. "I don't think she knows who Chris is."

Christmas morning Cissie said to me how nice she thought Chris was.

I replied somewhat casually, "Of course he is, he's your son."

Then she said, "Is he? I'm sorry I did not know him when he was a little boy."

I then asked her, "Cissie who am I?"

"You're my father," was her reply.

I went to the kitchen to help Chris and Tanya with Christmas dinner. And related my exchange with Chris's mother. He was shattered.

We were all shattered and escaped into discussion on how best to cook the bird. Chris and I agreed that wallowing in his mother's decline would do nothing for her and simply depress us. We had to carry on normally as best we could. If we were happy and engaged with Christmas our mood would affect Cissie positively as well. Dwelling on sadness was no good for anyone.

The Peking Circus is a more adult-oriented spectacle without clowns and animals. Rather it focuses on acrobatics and gymnastics at a level that is stupefying. The costumes and choreography are breathtaking. Cissie and I were thrilled at it and so were Chris and Tanya. I purchased the best seats in the indoor stadium-like theater. This was now my annual Christmas treat for the family.

However, this year Cissie did not "ooh" and "ah" as in past years. She sat quietly through the performance with little expression and no animation. She wasn't really there. As we walked out after the performance, Cissie talked to Chris as if he were a stranger. Then, Chris and Tanya took off on their own to explore Paris. Cissie and I went home on the metro. We walked quietly to the entrance and sat quietly on the train holding hands. I was distraught!

Chris and Tanya returned to London the next day. They were wonderful and we all put on the British stiff upper lip. But our sadness manifested itself in quiet farewells. Our friends had snapped a family photo of the four of us all dressed up on Christmas Eve. Tanya ran to a photo store to print the picture and bought a frame. She gave it to me before they left and I cried. The photo is still near my bed. It is a memorial to Cissie's last Christmas at home.

We went to a small Italian café for lunch after the kids had gone. It was near Cissie's favorite boutique. She loved the Italian designer Fabiana Filippi and I had promised her a Christmas gift from the store. We really enjoyed the café and conversed pleasantly. Cissie seemed quite normal.

I asked her again who I was.

And again she answered in the most matter-of-fact manner: "You are my father."

We walked to the boutique and selected fabulous winter slacks, sweater, and belt. Cissie entered the dressing room to try them on. She called me soon after to come in and help her. She was beginning to have trouble putting on her clothes.

They fit fine and she looked divine in them. We bought the clothes but clearly the sales lady noticed something was wrong with Madame.

And now the bottom fell out.

The next day, Cissie told me she wanted to go home. She had only come to this place for the festivities and now she wanted to return to her home in Gothenburg. She asked for her passport and started to pack. I told her she was home. This was her apartment in Passy. We had been living here for more than twenty years.

"Someone has fiendishly decorated it to look like my apartment but I would never live in a terrible neighborhood like this," she said. "And I have only been here a few days." I protested that we were in a very desirable neighborhood. She would have none of it.

Later, I asked how she would get home.

"In a taxi," she replied.

I countered that Gothenburg was a two-hour flight from Paris and further asked her for her address there. She could not say.

"Could it be Rue Raynouard?"

"Yes, that's it," she said.

This was our address in Passy. She insisted on having her passport. I had long taken possession of her identity papers and credit cards. She threatened to call the police and the Swedish Embassy and have me arrested. She tried to leave the apartment several times and I had to lock the front door to prevent her. This sent her into a rage. She demanded her wallet and credit cards and would not stop until I relented. Then she would hide them and I would spend hours looking for them. This went on for several days. I thought I was going to come apart.

Then her mood changed. It was New Year's Eve and I coaxed her into watching some of the festivities on TV. When we went to bed she snuggled up to me and we slept that way the entire night. We stayed that way in the morning as well.

Later that day she asked me, "Don't you think we should tell Chris?"

"Tell him what?"

"That we are living together and are in love."

"I think he knows that," I said.

She smiled. "I'm so glad we met."

On the first working day in January, I called the neurologist and related the most recent events. I was desperate for help and my nerves were shot. He insisted I give Cissie the antipsychotic pills for three days and call him then. The pills turned her into a lunatic, ransacking her closet, hiding stuff, and threatening to escape to her own apartment. Our friends from Christmas Eve came over and took us out to lunch, separately. We met afterwards and his wife looked frazzled.

I called the neurologist. He recalibrated the dosage of the new pills and we agreed if Cissie did not stabilize he would take her into the hospital for a full medical review. He was not happy about this because he feared that she would be further upset away from home. But he admitted we had little choice.

The adjusted dosage helped a bit but not enough. He decided to put Cissie in the hospital for one week beginning January 17. During our last days at home, we snuggled every night and she would tell me how much she loved me and that she had never been happier in her life. In the morning her mood was misery again. She would start crying and tell me that she did not want to live this way. "If I can't get better, I'll kill myself."

I reacted firmly that this was nonsense and she would get better. I knew her and feared this might not be an empty threat.

Two nights before the hospital date, we had a longstanding dinner with a French couple that we had not seen for months as they were away from Paris.

They were marvelous friends of many years and had written from Greece to express concern and support over my accident but I had not told them about Cissie. That morning I called them and told them about her. They didn't say much but suggested they bring an informal supper to us and I agreed.

Cissie was very pleased they were coming and dressed early. Her sense of time was deteriorating.

They arrived with a take out roasted chicken, celery remoularde, and slices of ham, roast beef, and cheese...and, of course, a baguette tradition. We opened a bottle of champagne in the kitchen.

Cissie said to our lady friend that she was so pleased to have them for dinner and apologized that she was unable to do it at her home. "This is not my apartment, you know."

Our friends, forewarned, played their parts graciously. They called the next morning and offered their full support.

Our last night at home, I cooked Cissie her favorite salmon and dill potatoes dinner. We had packed her bag in the afternoon. She wanted to go to the hospital. She knew she was sick and hoped they would make her better. The hospital admittance office scheduled us for a private room and midmorning arrival.

Chapter 20

The American Hospital of Paris

We checked into Cissie's room as planned; the nurse told us our doctor would see us later and that Cissie was scheduled for a series of medical tests in the afternoon as well as a visit from a psychiatrist who partnered with the neurologist. They would make adjustments to her antipsychotic dosage after their visits.

An attendant arrived to take Cissie's lunch order with two–three choices for each of three courses. We unpacked and she put on her hospital gown, etc.

Cissie weighed ninety-two pounds (forty-two kilos) at check-in. She had lost twenty-two pounds since Alzheimer's attacked, ten of which were lost in the last six months. She showed little interest in meals at AHP.

The first day went as planned. Cissie was relatively calm because she was kept busy with the tests and then the doctor visits. I stayed with her until after her dinner. She was anxious when I went home but took her medicine.

I arrived at 10:00 am the next morning and found her terribly agitated. She told me that the night nurse led a criminal gang of caregivers who took her to the airport where they kept their stolen goods and then tried to force her into prostitution with other patients. She refused to do this and tried to run away but they put her back in the room.

The psychiatrist arrived soon after. She thought maybe the new dosage was too strong. Cissie suffered delirium during the night. The neurologist decided to maintain the dosage for one more day.

For the two years prior to our arrival at The American Hospital of Paris, our neurologists had prescribed several daily medications for Cissie. The two principle ones were Exelon and Ebixa as an alternative. These were the only drugs considered serious candidates to slow the progress of Alzheimer's disease and were used worldwide. A round patch placed on the skin near the neck administered Exelon. It came in two sequential strengths to allow the body to build up to the medication. Every three days we had to move the patch to a different spot on her front and back.

I put the patches on for Cissie and moved them as instructed. She accepted them without complaint. Exelon did nothing for her but make her constipated and this she handled badly. She would get very upset and we went several times to the doctors for stronger prescriptions. Constipation was a known side effect but in Cissie's case diagnosis was more complicated because she ate very little by now and was losing weight.

She rejected the rationale that eating too little would make going to the bathroom more difficult for her. At one point the frustrated neurologist ordered an X-ray of her digestive track to prove to her she was not constipated. The radiologist confirmed that all was normal. Cissie was relieved but not really convinced.

We changed to Ebixa for several months with again no discernable results.

Our neurologist withdrew the drug in summer 2018. Social Security would no longer cover Exelon and Ebixa, as there was insufficient evidence to prove their value and certainly no evidence they helped Cissie. Happily, her constipation complaints lessened after we stopped the drugs.

Psychotics are prescribed to calm and control patients with advanced Alzheimer's but they have to be calibrated just right for each or they can have the reverse effect. These are powerful drugs administered for many mental disorders, not just Alzheimer's.

Now she was having a bad time with them at AHP.

It is still early days for medical solutions. I believe we will find a cure someday because the money, effort, and will are there to do so. But despite many trials and real investment, there are no proven drugs to either slow or reverse Alzheimer's at this time. I fear future advances will come too late for Cissie.

Cissie went crazy again on the second night at AHP and this time she wandered off. They found her at 3:00 am in her underwear in the hospital emergency room. The ER was far from her room—one floor down and quite a distance away. The night staff had no idea how she got there. The following morning I ordered a night guard who parked outside her room. Our neurologist lightened her dosage and conferred with his medical team. He asked to see me in his office at 7:00 pm.

I stayed with Cissie through her dinner at 6:00. She seemed a bit calmer and watched a little television...sort of. I gave her constant reassurance and professions of love. Then I went to see the neurologist. He was busy with patients and his office was somewhat chaotic. He was running late but asked me to wait. Finally, he called me in.

He came right to the point. "Mr. Barnet, you have to find a placement for your wife. She has severe Alzheimer's and cannot go home. She requires full-time care."

All along I knew this day would come and I knew I could not handle more of the home life since I returned from the orthopedic clinic. But I still balked. I froze with both my hands gripping his desk. He reached across and put his hands on mine with pressure.

"Listen to me!" he said firmly. "I cannot save your wife but I can save you! Look at yourself. You are on the verge of a breakdown. If you continue like this you will probably die. This is my opinion and this is the science. I'm telling you. You have to stop. You have continued longer than most spouses. You have done all you can and more. If you want to take care of your wife for the rest of her life, you have to stop now! Otherwise you will not live long enough to so do. Go home now, pour yourself a glass of wine, and eat something. I will arrange a meeting for you in the morning with the hospital's social services director. Come back to see me again at 7:00 pm. "

I knew he was right and he was right to order me to do this. I went home reeling and poured myself a stiff bourbon whiskey. On one hand I was relieved; on the other I was sadder than I had ever been in my life. Cissie would never see her beautiful home again and I was now alone. I called my son, Chris.

Chris had started advising me to put his mother in a home when he witnessed her behavior over Christmas. "Dad" he would say, frequently, "Mom has gone down way beyond what you can handle. You have been fantastic but now you have to think of yourself. I fully agree with the doctor. You have to take care of yourself now and you have to be strong. You have gone way beyond. Please follow his advice; I'm begging you. I love you and I don't want to lose you. I've lost my mother and I don't want to be an orphan."

The next morning I visited Cissie. She was relatively calm and very glad to see me. She was no longer running away at night but she still had her cell phone. She talked the night nurse into calling me at dawn to come get her out of this place and save her from the evil nurses. She could no longer figure out how to phone someone on her own.

I met with the social services director. The neurologist had briefed her and told me that the doctor was looking for an intermediate stage to regulate her medicine. He would explain all this in the evening. She informed me that proper facilities for Alzheimer's patients were generally full and it could take some time to get a place. She recommended an organization in Garches and La Celle Saint Cloud.

They were the best in the western suburbs and featured beautiful gardens. They also specialized in Alzheimer's disease. Most nursing homes had memory care units but did not specialize in this. I liked the idea of a near suburb location with the outdoor ambiance and particularly liked Garches. I had lived there as a boy and the American School was five minutes away. It was a twenty-minute drive from our apartment. Of course it had a waiting list.

The neurologist told me about the Clinic Rochebrune to whom he sent patients as a way station before they secured a placement. AHP was a short-stay hospital. Rochebrune was a new concept in France. It was designed as a geriatric/psychiatric clinic (small hospital) and had an Alzheimer's unit. They took patients for one month and used that time to confirm their diagnosis and regulate their medicines. From there they would move on to a memory care home or return to their family's care if that were warranted. He had secured a place there for Cissie and that should give me time to secure a home for her.

Cissie expected to go home and the doctor took responsibility to tell her about Rochebrune. Her moods changed daily and on the morning of her discharge she was in a happy state. She surprised me with her reaction to Rochebrune. The doctor made it sound great and she was excited about going there. So off we went by ambulance.

Chapter 21

The Clinique Rochebrune

Rochebrune is also in Garches in a residential area with a beautiful park. The memory unit was a lockdown with a geriatrist doctor, a psychiatrist, and a psychologist. Nurses and caregivers supported them. The unit had twenty or so private rooms and a common room where the patients sat in between activities and therapies arranged for them. This was my first exposure to a group afflicted with this disease. It is pretty depressing but Cissie did not seem to mind.

We settled into her dreary-looking room that she thought was fabulous. I was amazed. She met and interviewed with the medical team and answered their questions. *So far so good*, I thought. But when I got up to leave, she had a fit. She thought this was a day job for her to exercise and get fit. She wanted to return home in the evenings.

The doctor told me to say to Cissie whenever I left that I would be back soon and never anything more precise. Once said, depart immediately. It would be very difficult for her at first but then it would get easier. I left shattered as she sat alone in the common room with all these afflicted strangers. Some of them just sat with empty eyes. Few talked and then only if asked a direct question. Some were aggressive and stalked others, frequently trying to touch them and get into their rooms. One or two could get violent but not in a really dangerous way. Alzheimer's patients are rarely violent and the rare ones that are have to be isolated. Some talk to themselves or make irritating moaning or agitated sounds.

Cissie packed her bag every morning and sat with it in the common room waiting for me to pick her up to go home. When I arrived, the caregivers would take her bag back to her room and unpack it while I took her for a walk. After the first week they impounded her suitcase.

Chris came to visit his mother on her first weekend at Rochebrune. He had agreed with the neurologist that Cissie had to go into a home and kept telling me to be strong. We went first to visit the Alzheimer's home in Garches with a French friend. We came away impressed and started the process of securing a place for Cissie there. The French have a form for everything and without my French friend I don't think I could have completed the application. They thought they might have a place in three–four weeks but Cissie's acceptance would require the doctor's recommendation at Rochebrune and a concurring one with their psychologist at the home. He would interview Cissie toward the end of her evaluation period at Rochebrune.

Chris and I arrived at the clinic to visit Cissie and have lunch with her in their visitors' lounge. Rochebrune would let us take her out for lunch eventually but only after she had sufficiently acclimated to living there. After lunch we had a short walk in the garden and then sat with her in the common room for about thirty minutes. The doctor discouraged long visits.

It all went well and Chris was great with his mom. When it came time to go and she started to get up to leave with us, we gently told her she had to stay there. The look of growing alarm in her eyes unnerved Chris. When we got outside on the way to the car he doubled over and cried. Leaving mom was like shooting a puppy...impossibly cruel. We both wept. He never told me to be strong again.

Rochebrune had me meet with their medical team to determine my state of physical and mental health. They invited me to join their thirteen-week course to educate spouses. It was scheduled once a year beginning in March. The timing was good.

As the month at Rochebrune passed I became impressed with the whole place and particularly the medical team. The geriatric doctor was outstanding. She both confirmed Cissie's severe Alzheimer's and recommended her to the Residence Villa d'Epidaure. Thanks to The American Hospital and Rochebrune, we had found a good home for Cissie. Their psychologist interviewed her at Rochebrune. He was Belgian and spoke perfect English. He told Cissie all about Villa d'Epidaure, the people, the beautiful gardens, the hotel-like atmosphere, the activities. He determined that she was a good fit and excited her about the place. And I suspect his good looks, kind face, and charming manner gave her confidence. He impressed me and added to my confidence that Epidaure was the right place.

Rochebrune had both changed and recalibrated Cissie's medication. The purpose of these drugs is to calm patients and relieve their anxiety. The new formula seemed to work at this stage. Further, Cissie had regained some of her lost weight while there. The drugs stimulated her appetite and taking her meals with others made eating more enjoyable.

Beyond daily medical care and drug management Rochebrune provided physical therapy and entertainment to the memory care patients in the lockdown section of the hospital. A woman came twice a week to sing popular songs in a sing-along with the patients. There were arts and crafts and a caregiver read the daily newspapers to them every morning.

The medical staff met with me regularly to post me on Cissie's medical progress and her acclimation to her new environment.

During her last two weeks at Rochebrune I took her out to lunch in Saint Cloud next door, usually with friends who wanted to see her. Her oldest friend from SAS and Copenhagen came down with her husband. Cissie enjoyed these visits and outings. She no longer ate like a bird; now she ate like a horse.

Peter Barnet

Chapter 22

Residence Villa d'Epidaure

The psychologist at Rochebrune remarked to me, "We can do many things today but alas, we cannot journey through someone else's mind. We can analyze a person's behavior, understand their thinking, and even understand their thought process. But we cannot literally know what they are thinking. We cannot literally join their thoughts in process, the language in their heads. So patients still surprise us regularly."

Cissie was equally excited to leave Rochebrune to go to Villa d'Epidaure as she had been to leave AHP for this clinic. Kael, the young psychologist at the villa, had made it sound wonderful to her. Nevertheless, I marveled at her enthusiasm on both occasions. It was out of character for her.

A place opened up just in time at Epidaure. Cissie transferred there with Kael in an ambulance on February 18, 2019. I met them at the villa when they arrived.

Residence Villa d'Epidaure is a Greek style Mediterranean structure. It takes its name from a village south of Athens known for its health care. The villa is white with three floors above the ground floor. There are eighty-five single patient rooms. Each floor has approximately twenty-two rooms with a dining room and a common room for the residents. The atmosphere is light and cheery; the hallways are brightly lit. Everything is well maintained.

The ground floor has a sizable entrée area with lounge and front desk. It has a large common room that lets on a large garden with tables and chairs, chaises longues and walking space. The flowerbeds are large and filled with impatiens, petunias, and pansies. They are a sea of rainbow colors even in winter and add to a warm and inviting outdoor space. There is a smaller garden on the other side. Next to the entrance is the visitors' dining room that seats twelve.

The ground floor is really the public space of the villa including therapy rooms, hair salon, and medical offices. The housedog is a golden lab care dog named Hamlet and a loved member of the therapy team.

Epidaure greeted Cissie with a large sign on the front desk that said: "Welcome Maj Sigrid Barnet," her formal name. Kael chatted with her in the entrance lounge and then gave her a tour of the villa. I tagged along. He showed Cissie her room on the first floor next to the dining room that looked out on the garden. Her name plaque was already on the door. Finally he escorted us to the visitor's dining room. He had made a reservation for us at a table for two. He wished us bon appetite and said he would join us again after lunch.

Cissie took all of this well and seemed in good spirits. She liked Kael, which was enormous, as he would play the role of chief acclimation officer.

She enjoyed the lunch, a four-course meal consisting of a cold first course and a hot main course, followed by cheese and desert. This was the main meal of the day. They served flat and sparkling bottled water and a choice of white, red, and rose wine. They offered coffee and a chocolate at the end. Viva la France.

Kael returned at 2:00 pm. We had agreed that I should then make my goodbyes and he would spend more time with her largely in her room to familiarize her with it. Cissie started to panic but Kael distracted her. She followed him as instructed.

I visited Cissie five days a week at first and had lunch with her. She wanted to go home with me at the end of each visit. This damn near killed me. She was very lonely. Language was a major issue and the principal driver of my now-defunct plan to move to Sweden. Cissie simply refused to speak French and hadn't done so for over two years. She understood French but speaking took too much effort.

Several ladies on her floor and elsewhere greeted her with warmth but they soon backed off. They could not understand what she was saying in English. Cissie thought they did not like her. I talked to these ladies in French hoping they would still try to connect with Cissie. I failed. I would demonstrate to Cissie that the ladies liked her but couldn't understand her and this is why they did not react when she said hello. I begged her to speak a little French to them. I failed.

I enlisted Kael to help and he tried...but to no avail. He told me that as Cissie's disease advanced, nonverbal communications would become the norm for her as well as so many others. I knew this but it couldn't relieve her loneliness now.

The villa had a robust schedule of daily activities. Cissie took up painting and enjoyed it. She was pretty good at it and basked a bit in my compliments. Chris and I framed three and the villa hung them in her room. I knew painting was a good idea because of the following:

A friend and colleague in Paris, an extraordinary woman, had a mother in Chicago who suffered from Alzheimer's. She had been a known artist but when she started to struggle with the disease she gave it up. Eventually, my colleague put her in a home but did not like her lack of stimulation there. Then she had the idea to encourage her mother to paint again. She did and the results were striking.

My friend returned to Paris and made a documentary film about her mother and then published it in book form titled *I Remember Better When I Paint.* Cissie has benefitted from my colleague's initiative, as have Alzheimer's patients in care homes all over the world.

Cissie also loved to dance and gained an admiring public at afternoon tea dances. Music is major therapy for Alzheimer's victims, too. It was part of daily life at the villa. Beyond the tea dancing there were regular piano concerts and sing-alongs. Cissie loved the piano player and always wanted to sit as close to him as possible.

I attended a lecture at Villa Epidaure given by an organization that applies Montessori teaching techniques to Alzheimer's patients. Senora Montessori gained fame a century ago developing a method to educate troubled children effectively. One hundred years later we discovered that this method could be effective on impaired old people. Advanced Alzheimer's patients are often described as 8 year olds. This is why we used the term "second childhood" to describe senility before Alzheimer's breakthrough.

The lecturer used a case history to demonstrate how quality of life can be sustained in people one would think are better off dead. Her subject was a 90-year-old woman who was partially paralyzed and could not use one arm.

She sat in a wheelchair all day and did not move. She sat silently and without expression. The caregivers had pretty much given up trying "to entertain her."

The lecturer then demonstrated how they first interested the old lady in flowers and then taught her how to arrange them using her good arm. We watched her do this and witnessed her smile as she succeeded. They gave her back some quality of life. I was impressed.

Cissie tried to make friends with a man who spoke English...when he spoke. He was younger and spent his days walking the corridors alone or sitting by himself. She chased him a bit to make friends but eventually stopped. He simply could not communicate or react to others most of the time.

After six weeks or so, Epidaure gave me permission to take Cissie out for lunch and walks. There was little risk and she would no longer resist returning to the villa. That's why they do not allow this initially. Mostly we went out with friends at first and then it was a combination of friends and just the two of us. Her appetite was good. She restored all her lost weight and her slacks were getting tight. Her mood would vary daily.

I cut back visits to three times a week. Kael thought I should reduce to two and so did my psychologist in Paris. I came away upset after most visits because Cissie was so clinging to me and unhappy when I left. Kael kept telling me that I had to understand Cissie would forget about me leaving in a few minutes as her attention shifted to something else while I would feel bad about leaving her for the rest of the day. I knew he was right but I couldn't help it. I grieved for her everyday.

The thirteen-week course started at Rochebrune in March. We met at the clinic for three hours Wednesday mornings. The psychologist and a nurse led the group. They were professionals and kind. The group consisted of seven spouses. I was the only man. Three of us had partners in memory care homes including me; one still had a husband at Rochebrune and three husbands were at home.

We were all in our 70s or 80s.

Each session started with a PowerPoint presentation on the subject of the day followed by a group discussion. We covered all aspects of dementia and its variations. Alzheimer's accounts for 70% but others such as Louis Syndrome and Parkinson's are variations. They have specific symptoms and treatments but many similar to Alzheimer's, as well.

Subjects covered both the behavioral science that informs patient care and the medical science as we know it today, including physical changes and deterioration in the brain, treatments and medications, effects and side effects.

The most useful lectures detailed how the disease affects patient behavior over time and how to interact with them. Many of my instincts on how to interact with Cissie were logical to me but misguided in reality. For example, I always asked Cissie questions: "Who am I? Who is Chris?" to test her state of cognition. At Christmas she had not been able to identity us clearly. I learned never to ask her questions as this would stress her and make her feel inadequate. Today, I identify myself to her to avoid stressing her. Also, her calling me her father was probably her way of saying, "I know you are an important man in my life that I love and respect. It is easier for me to say 'father' than 'husband.'"

Further, I learned not to correct or criticize Cissie, never to make her feel she was failing. Always try to build the patient's self-esteem.

I learned that as the disease progresses nonverbal communication becomes more important than verbal discourse. Alzheimer's victims need social interaction but speech becomes more difficult and conversation becomes much, much more difficult. However, nonverbal communication prevents patients from feeling lonely and isolated. They can sit next to a "friend" at dinner and never talk but if the other person smiles to them and pats their hand or arm, for example, they are having an enjoyable social time. Conversely, if the person next to them is unhappy and irritated in their expressions, they will become nervous and unhappy, too.

There is a reason why we called senility second childhood. Alzheimer sufferers become emotionally and intellectually like 8 year olds. The malady robs them of their adult maturity.

Alzheimer's is essentially an old person's disease and it is exploding because we are living longer. However scientists believe that they may be able to identify young people who are genetically at risk of getting it years before it would appear. So, much development and testing is targeted to people in their 40s with the hope that if they can be identified there will be ways to protect them or reduce their odds of becoming victims.

What causes the plaques and tangles to grow in the brain that short-circuit and destroy cognitive nerves is unknown. We saw pictures of the changes in the brain as the disease progresses. They were terrifying. The advanced Alzheimer's brain looked to me as if it had been assaulted by a tiny machine gun or as if it were rotting. I felt the impact of those photos in my gut.

The course ended with lectures on how spouses should care for themselves given the terrible stresses involved with caregiving whether the patient was at home or in an institution.

We learned the importance of proper nutrition and good eating habits. A geriatric nutritionist taught us that after 70 our bodies require different foods and a variety of them daily. My reaction to her ideal daily diet was that she made sense but I would gain a lot of weight if I followed it religiously. Still, she gave us food for thought, no pun intended.

A physical therapist took us through stretching exercises to reduce stress and others to keep in shape.

Both the psychiatrist and geriatric internist interviewed us individually as they had before the start of the course. They updated their assessments on how we were doing and reemphasized our personal challenges.

The bottom line is that knowledge is essential to manage the realities of Alzheimer's and spousal care is equally important to patient care. When the neurologist had told me I had to separate from Cissie if I wanted to live long enough to care for her for the rest of her life, he was not kidding. The Rochebrune course added to that insight. Here is the syllabus of the course. There will be one like it wherever you live.

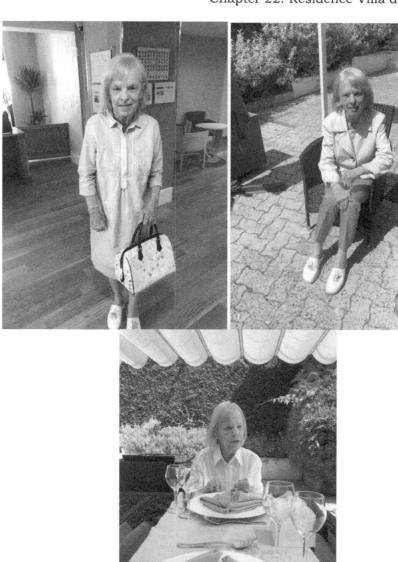

Cissie at La Villa d'Epidaure

Training Program for Spouses

- Better understand the disease: causes, evolution and treatments
- Communications and understanding how to maintain a dialogue with your spouse
- How to stimulate your spouse: fun and enjoyable activities to engage them
- Patient stresses and anxieties and how to help relieve them
- Caring for yourself: managing stress, recognizing exhaustion, and getting help
- Medical treatments for caregivers
- Nutrition: balanced diets for geriatric caregivers and patients
- The pleasures of eating and exercising
- How to sleep better
- How to make the patients' rooms at homes safe and secure for them
- The limits of home care and when to consider an institution for your spouse.

Our group discussions during and after the lectures were useful, too. This was in fact a support group. We were all in the same boat and picked up on the lectures to relate their relevance to our experiences with our spouses. Everyone wanted to tell their stories and responded to the ones of others. We were strangers but the reason for our gathering dissolved social barriers instantly, as is normally the case with therapy groups that share a common challenge.

I observed that each of us had individual experiences but the larger story was the same. They agreed.

My life now centered on visiting Cissie, attending the Rochebrune course, and putting our affairs in order. We had completed our wills, living wills, and powers of attorney on our last trip to the US in winter 2018. The wills and living wills were inactive as long as we lived outside the United States. Cissie and I were residents of France and therefore all legal matters had to comply with French law. The rules are different but the objectives are the same.

In France powers of attorney remain in force only as long as the person is competent to make decisions. There is a different mechanism to deal with incompetency and a specific process to exercise it. It is called a "mandate for future protection." Cissie and I signed these documents in 2011 that gave each other the sole responsibility for our affairs if one of us became incompetent. It is equivalent to a power of attorney and sadly it was now time to execute it.

The process required a court-appointed psychiatrist to certify that Cissie was now incompetent and to petition the local court to activate the mandate. This would give me operational control of Cissie's bank accounts and would give me the right to sell our assets, including our apartment. However, I could not close her accounts or complete the sale of the apartment without a final signature from the judge. This is a lengthy process in three stages but it is designed to protect the interests of the incompetent person.

By late spring daily life had its routine for Cissie. She had breakfast around 8:00 am and then remained in her room for her morning shower and dressed for the day. Sometimes she did this herself but more and more the caregivers helped her. She resented being washed by them when she neglected to do it and generally was not an easy patient.

Dressing herself was difficult. She would put her slacks on backwards with the fly and zipper on her backside. Somehow she could do it but it made going to the toilet awkward. Bras irritated her and she often tried to put them on upside down. Since she hated to be naked in front of the caregivers she often wore many layers of clothes to protect herself from them.

I would get upset regularly when I arrived for lunch to discover the state of her dress. The caregivers told me that it would upset her if they tried to correct her dress every day. So they let her put clothes on inside out, upside down, and turned around as long as it was not dangerous. She refused to let me re-dress her most of the time. She liked it that way. Yet if her outfit colors didn't coordinate, she would refuse to wear it. Cissie had not lost her sense of fashion or its importance to her.

...

Paris, June 1976

I was pooped. We had been shopping all day. We had left our hotel on Le Faubourg Saint Honore on the right bank at 10:00 am, taken the metro to the fashion boutique areas around rue de Reines on the left bank, and attacked them until 5:00 pm. We stopped briefly for a quick lunch. Paris was our last stop on our honeymoon for the sole purpose of shopping. This was the first of three days.

I was also puzzled. "Cissie, how come you haven't bought anything? I thought some of the clothes you tried on were divine on you, like that pink and gray blouse with the white slacks. You kept saying, 'we'll see.'"

"Oh, I had no intention of buying anything today. Today was research. Tomorrow we'll check out the right bank department stores and then go back to the boutiques. I always do it like this. I never buy the first things I see and like in case I find something I like even better. That's why I said we needed three days in Paris."

"Now I understand," I replied. "But how do you do this? I'm exhausted and not sure I'll survive two more days like this."

"Yes, you will, and you will be pleased when we're done. Shopping is an art and a science. You have to have an objective and a plan. I never buy a lot but I have to love what I buy. Everything has to work. That's the secret to being well-dressed."

We boarded Pan Am for the trip home with several outfits that were spectacular on Cissie. I was in awe and so proud of her and now she was my wife!

And that's how it continued over the years:

"What are you up to today, sweetie?"

"My girl friend and I are going shopping at Arlettie as usual. They are having a sale on Armani. Then we're going for lunch."

"That outlet center is going to put bronze statues of you two together in their entrance area one day. You are the discount twins and their patron saints."

"We don't buy much but we like shopping there and we have a good time."

"Have fun, Cissie, see you tonight."

...

Garches, May 2019

Three months in, the villa locked Cissie's closet because she would take all her clothes off hangers and stuff them in the bottom bin. It was chaos. She was constantly losing her things: clothes, watch, eyeglasses, shoes, belts, and handbags. Nothing was spared, including cosmetics and toiletries. I did not envy the caregivers. Happily the villa tagged all her things with her name. This was essential for the laundry service anyway and they could not reset her closet everyday. It was all so sad.

Then they took away her door key. The room door locking system made sense. The door could not lock from the inside so Cissie could not be locked in her room. It only locked on the outside so other patients could not go into her room uninvited.

This is a common problem in Alzheimer's facilities. Patients had their own key and the door locks were generic. Everyone had the same lock and the same key. This made access easy for the caregivers who had keys and replacing them easy if lost. Patients lost them regularly. Many wore their keys like a necklace hanging around their neck.

Cissie had trouble finding her room. When I took her back to it she was always nervous and wanted to go several times from downstairs to it for practice runs.

She could not remember the floor, the elevator button to push, or her room location. More and more she would say to me that she did not know she had a room. This would be her first time to see it. Then she would recognize it when we entered.

Many patients have the same problem and wander into other patients' rooms. One day the nurse called me at home. A man had hit Cissie in the face over her left eye. She was OK but very upset.

Evidently, Cissie unlocked and entered into what she thought was her room. She had gone to the wrong floor. She was shocked to find a man lying in her bed and tried to pull him out of it. He resisted and when Cissie persisted he hit her. The caregivers and the villa floor managers decided to take Cissie's key so she could not do this again. (Caregivers unlock room doors for patients who cannot manage keys.) I had to agree but it was awful and I felt so bad for Cissie. Happily she did not get a black eye and she did not remember the incident the next day.

The villa doctors had planned to lighten up Cissie's antipsychotic dosage once she acclimated to Epidaure. However, they continued and even strengthened the dosage a bit. They feared she would become too anxious and unruly if they reduced it. They further told me that her illness had advanced since her arrival.

Cissie stabilized over the summer but constantly complained to me that she was bored and wanted to go home. She was not doing well socially and her efforts to engage with others were often misunderstood as interruptive and rude. Kael spent a good amount of time helping Cissie through this rough patch.

Her false realities returned. She imagined she was always travelling or going out with girls on shopping trips and restaurant dinners. Most of these "imaginary events" were positive. Once she went to Lapland at the Swedish Artic Circle.

She told me it was too far and too cold so she had decided not to go there again.

Another time she and the girls went to that square with the restaurants. They went by train but there were none to bring them back. They walked and spent the night in the garden and it was raining. They all got soaking wet.

I never tried to correct her imaginary outings and travels. I think she invented them to relieve her boredom. Perhaps this was nature's way of easing her damaged mind. Also, they somehow connected her to her past life in Paris.

Cissie became harder to understand in the fall. She talked a lot and the doctor told me she would eventually enter the silent stage, but not yet. She started mixing Swedish and English and would describe goings-on in her mind unintelligibly. Increasingly, she could not find vocabulary to express her ideas. I did my best to encourage her to try without stressing her.

Chris called regularly and visited every six weeks. She loved seeing him but phone calls were now difficult for her so she cut them short.

She still knew my name and me and was as needy for me as ever. I constantly told her I loved her and she would say she loved me, too. But she could no longer remember Chris's name without prompting. He was that nice, good-looking younger man.

My routine continued three days a week with Cissie and as many lunch and dinner dates I could muster in Paris. All the doctors involved with our case advised me to return to as normal a life as possible and especially to avoid sitting home alone every night. They advised me that lunch dates were good but evenings with friends even better. I succeeded in two nights out a week and one lunch or so. I was happy to get invitations to dinner parties.

Nevertheless, I was lonely for the first time in my life. I had not lived alone for forty-three years. This was a major adjustment. I had spent many days and nights away on business and alone at night in hotel rooms, and I had lived alone when Cissie had attended Ritz Escoffier, but I had not been lonely. I always knew I would return to my family. They were always there.

Loneliness occurs when there is no one to come home to. I had enjoyed occasional evenings alone when Cissie had engagements with her ladies clubs and le Circle Suedoise. I could cook myself a steak and watch a movie. I enjoyed going to movies by myself. But these were little personal moments from daily-married life. Now there was no daily-married life anymore and I missed Cissie dreadfully. I stopped going to movies alone. They were no longer pauses but extensions of living alone. They enhanced loneliness.

I took one trip in April to the US to visit my brother and his family. His two daughters lived in Brooklyn and Wellesley, Massachusetts. They were married to great guys and had two children apiece. I really did not know my great nephews and niece and wanted them to know me before they grew up. This was a wonderful break from the sadness with Cissie. I adored my brother's grandkids. And always loved his daughters.

I thought I could not leave Cissie alone for more than a few days her first summer at Epidaure. She needed my company and I needed hers to make certain she was OK and to not feel so alone. I was relieved to have calm at home but I missed her and the apartment seemed empty, even desolate with out her presense.. Accordingly, I made no summer vacation plans and had little interest. I had not completely recovered from the accident and was reticent to drive distances.

Still, I traveled to London twice to see my son and his soon-to-be fiancée and once to visit our friends from the temporary apartment who had moved to Madrid. I accepted two weekend invitations from French friends in Le Touquet and the Dordogne. These were two–three nights away and did not interfere with my visiting frequency to see Cissie. I much appreciated them.

I sold our apartment in early July with a closing scheduled for early December. It was too big for me alone and filled with memories of Cissie.

I rented a smaller one not too far away. Renting made sense, as I wanted to stay flexible in case Chris decided to move back to the US. I would follow. However, he and his fiancée decided to stay in London for a few more years. That was OK, too.

I did not tell Cissie about the apartment sale. Why risk upsetting her?

They say the four most stressful events in life are death of a spouse, divorce, loss of a job, and moving. I had pretty much piled two of these into one year.

Chris and Tanya announced their engagement in the fall. This was a moment of joy for me in an awful year. They made a great couple and illustrated the continuous rebirth of life. Cissie and I were yesterday's news; Chris and Tanya were tomorrow's news and that was as it should be. Sad endings offset by happy beginnings. And they wanted children!

We agreed they would come for Christmas and we would tell Cissie then. We made reservations for lunch on Christmas Eve in Boulogne near Epidaure in Garches and Christmas Day at a famous brasserie at Bastille. It was all we could do. The caregivers dressed Cissie in her elegant clothes and off we went in our little Mini. We gave her gifts and read her cards to her and tried to make her feel the center of attention. Cissie had a good time at both lunches and seemed pleased with their news.

Chris and Tanya planned their wedding celebrations over a weekend at a Chateau outside Toulouse with about fifty guests. They would marry legally in London prior to the big weekend in France. Sadly, it was impossible for Cissie to attend. We decided that they would come to Paris for a wedding luncheon at a lovely place in the park prior to going down to Toulouse. We would tell Cissie that Chris and Tanya had decided on no wedding festivities; they preferred to spend their money on a fabulous honeymoon and they were going to Le Cote d'Azur the next day.

Cissie reacted, "I think you are smart. Spending a lot of money on a big wedding doesn't make sense. Why, you could spend $5000 on something like that."

We agreed. Later we laughed about her remark. But it was so sad.

I tried to help Cissie make friends on each visit to her. I figured I had to make them my friends, too. If they liked me maybe they would spend more time with Cissie despite the language barrier. Alzheimer's sufferers need love and good cheer. They react with smiles when others behave this way...and they get nervous if others are cold and angry or irritated. I greeted many with big hellos, kissed a lot of cheeks a la Francaise, and waved to others who were sitting in the big downstairs lounge. They always returned the greeting and brightened when they saw me.

Cissie referred to ladies she thought were socially important to her as "Kerstin." This is a common Swedish name. She called anyone interesting to her "Kerstin" and thought they were Swedish. Of course, they were French with names such as Nadine, Veronique, and Caroline. There were no Kerstins at Villa d'Epidaure.

I always greeted Cissie with a big, almost theatrical hello: "HI CISSIE, C'EST MOI, YOUR HUSBAND, PETER. HOW'S MY BEAUTIFUL GIRL TODAY?"

I did this for two reasons: to bring good cheer and to make it easier for Cissie to remember who I was. Sometimes she would react with relief: "Thank god you're here!" Sometimes she was expressionless. It varied daily. She talked about me to other patients and caregivers a lot, combating her loneliness, I imagine. We became known personalities as a result.

However, if I engaged with her "friends" in the lounge or other family members in the visitors' dining room she became irritated and pulled me away. She wanted me to herself, as our time together was so precious to her. I understood this but feared others might have felt a bit slighted. Most visitors comported themselves in an upbeat manner. But many spouses would start to whimper at the end of their lunch if their loved one left to go to the bathroom across the hall. On many afternoons I would leave Cissie (never easy), get into the car, and start whimpering, too.

The cruelty of Alzheimer's for me is I have lost my wife but there is no closure.

I discussed this with the doctor at Villa Epidaure. He told me, "The human mind likes clarity. Losing one's spouse to death is clear. You know she is gone. You will never see her again and you will talk to her only in your mind and through your memories. You will grieve but eventually recover. Death is closure."

Alzheimer's prevents closure because your husband or wife is still there. It condemns the spouse to what the French call le deuil blanc—white grieving or never-ending grieving. My friend in Montana describes every visit to his wife as like pulling a Band-Aid off a scab and reopening the wound. I agree.

At Villa Epidaure, I confirmed a growing belief that we are not the best caregivers for our spouses because we are emotionally involved. They will be better cared for by professionals. Doctors do not like to treat their family members because they are emotionally involved. They cannot be objective. I believe the same applies here. Professionals are not emotionally involved and are trained to follow proven protocols. Some may lack empathy but if they are good at their craft, they will be better than us.

It is humanly impossible not to lose patience with your spouse as the disease advances. Spending hours each day helping them find things they have lost, misplaced, or hidden takes its toll for starters. We are forced to correct them a lot and inadvertently point out their mistakes. They fail every day at home.

They do not fail at Villa Epidaure; no one is critical or corrects patients at the home. Everyone succeeds and his or her efforts are applauded. At home they are losers; at Epidaure they are winners. Cissie regained weight and though heavily drugged she regained some self-esteem. She is famous for her dancing at Epidaure (she always was a great dancer) and we have framed three of her paintings. She is proud of them. We are proud of her. This is terribly important to boost her quality of life.

...

New York, November 1978

"Ladies and gentlemen, please take your places for the tango competition this evening. Our judges will tap those couples that are out during the competition until one is left dancing and declared the winner. It doesn't matter if you have never tangoed. Give it a whirl."

A sea of men in black tuxedos and a few in white tie tails and their ladies in floor length evening dresses flooded onto the enormous dance floor. Dressing up was part of the fun and everyone looked great. I escorted Cissie onto the floor. She was dressed in a stunning black Escada ensemble with gold brocade accents. She looked ravishing. *Move over, Grace Kelly,* I thought.

Our friends from the singles group houses in the Hamptons organized a formal dinner dance cotillion at The Roosevelt Hotel just for fun—a chance to keep summer society going in the off-season. It was a wildly popular idea and required the huge Grand Ballroom of the Roosevelt to accommodate the group.

"Peter, do you know how to tango?" Cissie said excitedly. "I don't think I've ever done it."

"Yes, a few times," I replied. "It's not hard, three steps forward for me, backwards for you, and then a turn around and another three steps. Arms held out like an exaggerated foxtrot stance and cheek to cheek like Latin lovers."

Cissie picked it up right away. We really had a good time doing it. One by one couples were tapped out but we were sort of oblivious to the others. We were having so much fun.

Suddenly, Cissie whispered breathlessly in my ear. "Be cool, don't react but I think we are almost alone out here."

I obeyed.

The judges came over to us clapping and the music stopped thirty seconds later.

We looked around. We were alone on the dance floor. Everyone was clapping. We couldn't believe it. We had won. Cissie looked radiant and so did I. I think we were sort of disbelievingly proud of ourselves.

We never forgot that evening. It was a shining reminder of our youth and Cissie's beauty.

...

Paris, November 2019

I was determined to make 2020 a new year. 2019 had been about Cissie; 2020 had to be more about me. I booked a four-week vacation in the US beginning in mid-January. The doctors all encouraged me to do this and so did my family and friends. This would be the first time I would be away from Cissie for more than four–five days. Kael suggested I call Cissie every two days. I think he felt I needed to do that. He promised to take good care of her in my absence and knew how to reach me, of course.

So, off I went first to Palm Beach to visit my brother and perennial friends, then to Montecito California to visit my oldest friend and his wife, and finally to a five-day stay at The Yale Club in New York. The Club had become "my home" in the US. It was my roots.

The doctors were right; a long vacation was a good idea. I got away from caregiving and returned to normal activities and normal conversations with people who were important to me. I spoke to Cissie every two days.

She would say, "Oh thank god you called! Peter, you have to come right away."

I reminded her that I was in New York on university business and for our personal affaires, too. I assured her that I missed her and loved her and would be back soon.

I avoided telling Cissie that I was touring the US visiting our oldest friends. That might have upset her. She could always understand business trips. I returned to Paris February 6 but planned to go back to the US in April to visit more friends. Of course, this did not happen.

Chapter 23

Covid-19

Villa d'Epidaure went into self-quarantine on March 10, 2020 one week before the French government ordered the closing of schools followed by two months of national lockdown at this writing. The world discovered Zoom and distance everything. I could not visit Cissie and telephone calls were restricted to not overwhelm the switchboard. Twelve out of eighty-five patients tested positive and all residents were restricted to their single rooms, including taking their meals alone in them.

Cissie's isolation and our restricted communications ratcheted up my normal worries about her but she managed well thanks to excellent care at the home. Her fantasy world kept her busy in her mind and lessened her boredom and feelings of loneliness. I could not see her for three months. She tested negative for the virus.

I joined a regular support group sponsored by Alzheimer's France in November 2019. The disease has become prevalent among expatriot groups as well and this was their pilot for Americans and other anglophones in English. My friend who discovered painting as therapy and several other American ladies, some touched by ths disease worked with Alzheimer's France to accomplish this. It has been a success and I am in their debt. We meet or Zoom once a week.

Support groups are essential. Alzheimer's support groups are Weight Watchers and Alcoholics Anonymous on steroids. They play the same role of helping people cope with serious challenges by bonding together, sharing common challenges and experiences, and comforting each other. They differ in that they are not dealing with personal physical or psychological afflictions. They deal with the loss of a spouse who is still alive.

My support group comprises five women and me. They all have different stories. Some are in later-in-life marriages. They had found companions with whom to enjoy their golden years. Now they are fulltime caregivers. That was not the idea and they do not feel cut out for it. Others have an age gap with their sick husband. Some have experienced the terror of looking for their spouse who just took off one day. One time, a husband in question went for a walk in Paris and ended up two kilometers away in Boulogne. His wife told the group that she called around to police stations and finally found him. That's life-shortening stress.

Several in the group sleep with their house keys under their pillows and the front doors locked.

One husband fell and broke his hip during a vacation in a small town in August. This is not a good month for emergency surgery in a seaside village in France...and for a seriously impaired old man. She got through it and I marveled at her resilience.

One member just put her husband in a home and is suffering the conflicting emotions of liberation and guilt. We all tell her she has done more than enough and she should not feel guilty.

When we meet, everyone expresses a gamut of emotions from frustrated to frantic, anger to exhaustion, and most signal that occasionally they are overwhelmed. But they motor on. They have no choice. They do what they have to do. I learn a lot at each meeting about the strength of the human spirit.

In June, I visited Cissie at Villa d'Epidaure for the first time in three months since the corona virus lockdown. I wore a mask and entered from the garden into an isolated space where we could meet and maintain social distancing.

She sat at a big table and watched me without expression as I approached.

"Hello, I'm Cissie Barnet," she said.

"Hello, and I'm Peter Barnet, your husband," I replied.

"No you're not."

"Yes, I am." I took off my mask.

"Oh, you sort of look like Peter. And your blazer looks familiar."

I was so happy to see Cissie and we reestablished our forty-four year marriage.

After awhile, with a little coaxing, she gave me a smile.

Lessons Learned

One word describes Alzheimer's disease: "cruel." It destroys the sufferer's mind. It does it slowly and relentlessly. Gradually the person disappears. It offers no hope of recovery and for the couple it changes the calculus of old age. It upends their retirement dreams and plans. It destroys their ability to enjoy their golden years. It affects the whole family. It crushes the soul.

That said, I've tried to distill a few lessons learned that may hopefully be of help to others in my situation.

1. The emotional toll is higher on the spouse than on the children of an Alzheimer's victim. That's why doctors treat the couple because the healthy spouse is at greater risk of mortality than the victim. No such risk applies to the children. This makes sense because the relationships are obviously different.

2. Spouses are often critical of their children not doing enough to help. But it is normal that they do less. Most probably they do not live with their parents and have their own families and careers. They are likely less invested in their parents than spouses are with their husbands and wives.

3. Alzheimer's is probably easier on the victim than on the spouse. Their damaged minds protect them from cognitive misery as the disease progresses. No such protection exists for healthy minds, which is why we are at risk.

4. Intellectually, it is not difficult to understand the right things to do. However, emotionally they are difficult to live with. Looking back, my decision to put Cissie in a home was not hard; it was

the only decision. The hard part has been living with it emotionally. Everyone is different but it helps to see a psychologist regularly, join a support group, maintain your social life, and pursue interests that you like and do well. These are the stuff of normal life that makes old age meaningful. They will not erase the emotional burden of loving caregiving but they will make it easier and safer for you.

5. Many caregivers express feeling of guilt if they lose patience with their spouses at home or if they have put them into memory care. Psychologists try to help them conquer those feelings but it's not easy because our basic emotions tend to override our intellectual understanding.

6. It is not selfish to want to salvage what is left of your life, but again emotions can make this feeling difficult to dismiss. Psychologists will tell you that doing something for yourself doesn't mean it is at the expense of your ailing spouse. Of course, they are right. It's yourself you have to convince. I keep telling myself this everyday. It helps.

7. Outbursts of anger and then feelings of shame do not make you a bad person. They make you a human being who cares.

8. Drugs and particularly antipsychotics are a regular necessity to treating Alzheimer patients. Tranquilizers and sleeping aids also play a role. Nobody likes these medications but they serve two fundamental purposes: they spare the victim high anxiety and calm them sufficiently to manage their care.

9. Despite drugs, patients have good moods and bad like everyone else. When your partner is anxious and complaining to you, change the subject to happy things. Alzheimer's victims, like children, are easily distracted. If they want you to solve a problem for them, tell them you will. Nonverbal communications are critical, too, and particularly when real conversation is no longer possible for the victim. You may be bored sitting silently with your spouse but they are not bored sitting with you and are happy when you physically telegraph love and affection.

10. Your own denial is normal in the early stages and Alzheimer's is difficult to diagnose. But refusing to recognize the situation can become a serious problem the longer it is put off. It will frustrate the entire family, endanger the victim, and could be harmful to you.

11. Don't hide the truth from friends too long. As soon as social life has to change and symptoms start to appear, inform them. Otherwise they will wonder why you seem antisocial. Tell them and they will support you. Support from friends is vital to manage and cope with this disease. It's particularly vital to you.

12. Planning ahead is essential. It gives you options and time to put well thought through action steps in place. Make certain your financial and legal affairs are in order. Don't try to do it all yourself; get help from experts and help from friends. You will live longer.

13. Don't be afraid to cry when alone or with your support group and your psychologist. Crying is like a steam valve. It lets out the stress and restores much needed calm. My psychologist repeatedly told me to cry.

13. And you have to laugh. Laughter and humor help us cope with the incopable. The situation is terribly sad but if you cannot laugh or make jokes, the sadness can overwhelm. I've always believed that life is much too serious to be taken seriously. Humor keeps us going...at least it does for me.

Peter Barnet

A Final Word About Cissie

I began writing this book as therapy for me and as a helpful guide for those who might find themselves in this same boat some day. As such I intended it as a useful exercise for me and for future primary caregivers. As I wrote it, I came to realize that this story is also my tribute to Cissie. How could it not be?

Cissie is or was a remarkable woman. She had many talents, she had many gifts, and she was a great beauty. She wanted a bigger, broader, and more challenging life than that afforded by her circumstances and life in Gothenburg when she came of age.

She had the independence and strength of character to strike out alone to achieve it. She knew her own mind and she was willing to take the good and the bad from her decisions. Yet she never denied her roots or loyalty to Sweden and its culture. In fact, her expatriate life enhanced her patriotism.

She possessed a natural stoicism. She could take a beating and keep on going. Her thirty-year battle with rheumatoid arthritis was heroic. She was fiercely loyal to me. She was often critical of me, too, as she was of so many things and so many people. But she had a good heart and would do anything for those she loved. She stayed by my side through good times and bad.

Cissie lost her last battle with Alzheimer's. She could not win it; no one can, at least not yet. But on net she had a great life filled with interesting people, places and achievements. She used her considerable gifts well. She enjoyed her life and she never bored me. She never bored anyone.

Peter Barnet

A Final Word About Me

What is the old saying about adversity? "If it doesn't kill you, it makes you stronger." I guess that's right. I hope that's right. My war against my wife's Alzheimer's is now six years old. It has eaten up those years and introduced me for the first time to feelings of despair. Yet I have remained positive. I have a "glass is half full" mentality, which is useful when fighting this dreadful disease.

I miss Cissie every day and feel so bad for her that she was cheated out of her old age. And when I think this way, I despair. But when I think of the life we have had together, I am grateful for it. And when I think of my son, Chris, and his now wife, Tanya, I smile. They want children and I want a grandchild.

Life is regenerating, as it should.

Thus, there is much to live for and enjoy. I would not change the life Cissie and I had together and I shall always love her. She was one hell of a woman. So I will continue to suffer le deuil blanc but revel in the joy of Chris and Tanya and of my brother, his family, and my friends. Life is not over and, as Humphrey Bogart says to Ingrid Bergman as they parted for noble purposes in the final scene of the film, Casablanca: Cissie, "we'll always have Paris" and we'll always have the music from "A Man and a Woman." "Here's looking at you, kid."

Peter Barnet

Peter Barnet

Acknowledgements

When I reflect on our expatriot lives together, it is fair to say Cissie and I have friends everywhere but not a lot of friends in any one place. I doubt I could have written this book without the support of our friends throughout this challenging time for us both. I doubt I would have had the strength and might not have survived. I owe them my sanity and they will always have my gratitude and love.

And a special thanks to my brother, Bruce, and my son, Christopher. With them on my team, how could I not come through?

And another special thanks to my friend, Barry Lando, who is a reputed journalist and served as my editor. His counsel was invaluable. I shall always be grateful for his friendship and assistance.

Made in the USA
Las Vegas, NV
09 December 2021

36788644R00085